Pet Pig

Keeping Pigs as Pets

Pig book for care, training, health, grooming, costs and feeding.

by

John Jepperton

Disclaimer

Published by : IMB Publishing 2015

Table of Contents

8

Foreword

Are you looking for an unconventional pet to show off? Do you want an intelligent companion that can take care of itself without demanding significant maintenance efforts? Have you ever considered pigs as pets?

If your answers to any of these questions are in the affirmative, you might actually want to consider getting a pig as a pet. They are fat and gullible beings who like gobbling up anything they are given. They are absolutely adorable and friendly – the kind you'd like to see when you come home after a long day!

Wondering how having a pig as a pet differs from other animals? It is actually pretty simple and similar. Everything you need to know about pigs is contained here!

From a basic introduction to different pig breeds to their training needs and grooming concerns; everything is covered here in ample detail. If you are new to this animal or if you are looking for ways to improve your experience as a pig owner, this book will prove to be an unparalleled asset for you!

So leave your worries behind and embark on a promising journey with your snout-y companion! Read through this book carefully to understand how you can pet pigs for greater gains! It's up for grabs!

Chapter 1: Introduction

Having an animal as a pet is one of the most rewarding activities you can indulge in. Even with all the pampering and caring you need to do for your pet, you feel good inside.

They accompany you through the thick and thin. And for the most part, pets are the most reliable and consistent companions you will be encountering in your life!

There are quite a few animals that can be taken in as pets. Cats and dogs are the two most common house pets on earth. In fact, about 47% of households in the United States alone are known to own dogs while over 37% have cats. And these statistics don't yet include the proportion of households that opt for multiple pets!

Given the numbers, you might want to try out something new. Anyone can have a cat or a dog! Is it really that simple with a pet pig?!

Pigs are generally amiable creatures. They like being pampered and would eat almost anything that is offered to them. They can get pretty randy if left alone for too long or given a free range. Nevertheless, most people find pigs to be much easier pets than dogs or cats.

Pigs can be broadly categorized into two groups; the wild pigs and the domesticated ones. Naturally, your first preference should be small domestic pigs – especially if you are new to it. They grow readily in size so you need to develop the required contingencies earlier on!

As long as you are giving it all that it needs, you wouldn't come across any problems. Pigs are infinitely different from dogs and cats when it comes to reciprocation of feelings. They also differ considerably in terms of show animals.

It is important for you to be absolutely sure about your choice of animal before you head out to purchase one. The association cannot be lost overnight; if you are ready to share your house with a pig for no less than two decades, this pet will prove to be an awesome addition to your family!

Keep in mind that having a pig as pet is different from other animals. The good thing is; you can find all relevant information here. Keep reading to find out how you can pet a pig for greater gains!

Chapter 2: The "Oink Oink-ing" Pet

The cat meows, the dog barks and the pig oinks. It is the specific noise that they make to interact with their surroundings. If you've ever been to the farmhouse or a place with pigs, you might already be familiar with its sound. The noise is typical of a pig; if you are bothered by it, you might want to reconsider your decision!

But apart from that, there are quite a few things about the pig, which makes it a worthy companion. In fact, quite a few people changed their perceptions about a pig after having it as a pet.

Here are some of the facts about keeping pigs as pets that might convince you to try it out. Don't rush yet; there is a lot to be learned before you can actually head out to buy one!

1) Some Facts about Pigs

Here are some interesting facts about pigs that may fascinate you. You are advised to read these at your own risk – you might want to head out and buy a pig straight away! So here it goes!

1. Pigs Converse! They have a series of oinks, grunts and squeals which signify different emotions!
2. Pigs are intelligent. In fact, they are often regarded as more intelligible species as compared with the children under the age of three, dogs, cats and other animals!
3. Contrary to popular belief, pigs are clean animals. They like keeping their sleep area spotless and would usually head out to relieve. They are extremely easy to potty train – or more like, they are naturally potty trained!
4. They are generally social and peaceful creatures. They like mixing with other animals but do particularly well with their own kind. They generally do not get aggressive, though if

they are left alone for too long, they might become reserved and unhappy.

5. They get affected by the seasons and it shows in their behavior. They tend to be excited and hyped up during the summer season while the winters are slow, depressing and irritable for them. An irresponsive pig especially during the winters is a sign of normalcy!

6. The Chinese Zodiac has it too! The pig represents happiness, fortune, virility and honesty!

7. The pig is an essential part of the ecological system. They help build new plant colonies and spread seeds and pollens. Their rooting behavior disturbs the soil to provide favorable conditions for the new plants to grow.

8. Pigs are omnivores. In fact, they would gobble up just about anything you hand out to them. Be mindful of your fingers; you don't want them to be near their food while they are feeding!

9. According to their body size, pigs have small lungs. Even the slightest hint of a lung disease can kill it!

10. Most pigs that are slain for food are about six months old. This means they are deprived of at least 95% of their lifespan!

11. A famous British writer (who also served as the Prime Minister twice during the 20th century) praised the pig species in the following words, "*Dogs Look Up To Man. Cats Look Down To Man. Pigs Look Us Straight In The Eye And See An Equal!*"

12. Pigs have good memory and sense of direction. They can find their way back home over extremely large distances as well.

13. Like dogs, pigs are known to be saviors as well. Although this particular aspect about pigs is not popular, there have been instances where a pig helped its master escape a horrible accidental death! It substantiates the intelligence claims!

Most of these facts are common while some might not really be so. If you find the idea of keeping a pig as a pet fascinating, the next section will give you more reasons why you should try it out! Keep reading to find out everything you need to know about keeping pigs as pets!

2) Should You Consider Getting a Pig for a Pet?

It is almost like asking whether you should get a dog for a pet or not; there is no generalized answer to the question. It all depends on you whether you'd like to take one in or not.

However, there are a few other considerations you will need to take into account before moving forward with your decision.

For the most part, pigs are amiable beings. But in some countries and regions, keeping pigs as pets is not considered legal. For instance, across several regions in Australia, keeping pigs as pets – even in the backyard – is strictly forbidden.

In other areas, you might need special permits in order to walk your pet pig or have it transported to any other place. Make sure you check in with the laws of your region before opting to purchase a pig. If it isn't legal, it will only get you into trouble!

Besides this, there may be other restrictions with respect to their upkeep. For instance, the government might impose certain restrictions about what the pigs are to be fed or what they shouldn't be fed.

Moreover, some laws prohibit the burial of a pig. Go through all the rules and regulations pertaining to pigs in your region before you get one.

Another important consideration you need to take into account is this; will you be able to give it the time and affection required to keep it from becoming violent?

A pig who feels neglected may transform into a monstrous creature. It may not be apparent from their innocent faces but they have the capacity to create havoc in your house.

If you are too busy to give it time, you can try buying two pigs to keep each other company. If that is too expensive, the next best option is to leave this job to those who are well-suited for it!

Keep in mind that you will need to get your pig tattooed in the ear or add an identification tag to it. It is ordained by law to brand your pig so that it can be identified if and when the need arises!

The pigs like to snuggle up with their owners. Besides this, their rooting instincts cannot be stopped. If you have any reservations about the natural lifestyle of a pig, it is advised for you not to try keeping it as a pet.

The pig does not become "cultured" simply because it is being brought up in a home. It will behave more or less the same way as it would on a farm or in the wild.

It will consume anything and everything that is lying strewn across the floor (or any other place where it can reach) – this includes debris and garbage of all sorts. If this is not the kind of behavior you expect from your pet, well then, it is pointless to pursue keeping a pig as a pet!

The choice is yours to make! If you can keep up with an unconventional pet that has its specific needs, keeping a pig as a pet may be a good idea. It usually works out well for people.

Whether it will do the same for you or not; this depends on your willingness to accommodate a stout little creature in your house and your life!

Chapter 3: All about Breeds

There are a lot of things you need to take into consideration while looking out for a pet. It is important for you to understand that such an association usually lasts for decades.

So if you are merely hoping to "try" it out or if you are looking for a short term pet, make sure you have the relevant contingencies planned. You cannot simply put a pet out because you can no longer care for it! Animal Rights' agencies are quite active these days. You definitely don't want to get on their wrong side!

Once you've decided about getting a pig for a pet, the next thing you need to figure out is - which one?

This section talks about how you should select a pig. It shouldn't be random; you need to know exactly what you are getting yourself into! Read through carefully – it will make a lot of difference to your adventurous journey!

1) Pigs Have Breeds Too?

Yes! Like dogs and cats, pigs have breeds too. This is the reason why you see diversity in their colors, sizes and temperaments. While some breeds are easy to pet and care for, some might prove to be quite a handful. So you need to do your research about the pig breed which suits you best!

There are quite a few pig breeds out there. Like cats and dogs, their pedigree database is exhaustive. However, there are few associations that document this species because they are essentially classified as livestock.

Nevertheless, there are a handful of exceptionally popular pig breeds you will be interested in. We'll be covering these to limit the scope of our debate and choices.

The Berkshire

It is one of the oldest registered pedigree breed for pigs originating from the United Kingdom. It is classified as a medium to large animal, averaging at about 600 pounds in weight. It is primarily black colored with a few white patches. It has a short snout and muscular build with erect ears. They are usually friendly and curious. The purity of this breed can be confirmed from the ABA (American Berkshire Association) and The British Pig Association. This breed was popular for the purpose of consumption. However, they are increasingly being taken in as pets in different parts of the world. Apart from their humongous weight, they pose few challenges as pets!

The Mule foot

The Mule foot is generally of a solid black color though few white spots are considered acceptable for this breed. It is believed to have originated from the Gulf Coast. As compared with the Berkshire, they have drooping ears – though their ears should not fall into the face. The breed received its name from the characteristic non-cloven hooves. They typically weigh between 400 and 600 pounds – equivalent to the Berkshire. It is one of the popular domestic breeds that are being selectively bred by reputable breeders these days!

The Tamworth

The Tamworth is solid red in color. It originated in the United Kingdom as well. Black spots on the Tamworth are considered objectionable. They have a fine and soft hairy coat with large erect ears across a slightly dished face. They are intelligent breeds that have the capability of adjusting to varied climates. The red coat offers protection against sun burn. They typically weigh between 400 pounds to 600 pounds and are classified as medium sized animals.

The Large Black

As the name suggests, they are solid black in color and are typically larger than most other breeds. A mature Large Black weighs about 600 to 800 pounds and is therefore classified as a large animal. It originated in the United Kingdom though there are at least 300 breeders outside the native country involved with this breed. They have large ears that cover the eyes. Besides this, the Large Black is typically longer and has a deep body. They are known to produce a large litter. Although a little difficult to find, the Large Black is undoubtedly one of the most amazing breeds you can have as pets.

The Hereford

The Hereford is a unique pig that originated in the United States. It is a red and white colored pig with small erect ears and a long slender body. A mature Hereford weighs about 400 to 820 pounds and is therefore considered as a medium to large sized animal. There are strict guidelines with respect to the Hereford's color. Its face needs to be at least $2/3^{rd}$ parts white and its body has to be $2/3^{rd}$ parts red in order to be classified as a Hereford. This particular breed has been through significant crossbreeding, inbreeding, interbreeding and other breeding practices to create a superior pig breed. This explains its resemblance with other breeds like Duroc, Poland China, and others.

The Poland China

This breed can be roughly traced back to Ohio in the United States although their origin is not very clear. The Poland China (which does not follow its name) is primarily black in color with distinctive white spots on the face, feet and the back. If the Poland China has more than one feet of solid black color, they are disqualified from the group according to the rules.

They have small floppy ears that droop into its face. Besides this, the Poland China cannot have any other colors in the coat. The Poland China has striking resemblance to the Berkshire. Make sure about your pig's breed before you intend to purchase it.

The Chester White

The Chester White is strictly white in color that segues into a light pink. The presence of any other color on its coat makes it eligible for disqualification. The breed is known to have originated from Pennsylvania, United States. It has a slightly dished face with floppy ears that do not fall into the eyes, and a characteristic thick white coat. The white color puts it at an elevated risk of sunburn so you need to build a summer shelter for it. Apart from this, the Chester White is known for its long life span, muscle gain and medium size.

The Landrace

The Landrace is believed to be the fifth most recorded swine breed. It also possesses a white coat though minor color variations are accepted. It has floppy ears that cover its eyes and stretches almost parallel to its snout. The Landrace is one of the most localized breeds. You'll come across the American Landrace, the British Landrace, the Belgian Landrace, the Danish Landrace, the Dutch Landrace, the French Landrace, the German Landrace, and several other localized breeds. There are little variations between these breeds. However, each has adapted to the local climate and hence has an improved lifespan in the native region.

The Hampshire

The Hampshire has a black and white coat. It is believed to have originated in the United Kingdom though it has gained massive popularity in the United States over the previous years. The Hampshire is primarily black in color with a distinctive white belt encompassing the body completely including the front legs. They have erect ears and a characteristically curly tail.

The Hampshire becomes eligible for disqualification if it has white colored spots across the face or the rear half of the body. Similarly, black spots on the white belt are considered for disqualification. The specific pattern of colors on its coat differentiates it from other breeds.

The Duroc

The Duroc is a red colored swine. Significant white or black markings on the coat disqualify it from the breed. They have droopy ears that fall over the eyes. The Duroc is believed to have originated from the United States and has gained popularity globally for its rich color and structure.

The Duroc is heavy boned and firm footed. Its coat colors may vary across darker shades of red. It may be confused with Tamworth and Hereford because of the striking resemblance in coat colors. However, the Duroc is naturally prone to ridging and typically has less than six udder sections on the underline. Hence, these can be differentiated from similar looking breeds easily.

The Yorkshire

The Yorkshire is also one of the most popular pig breeds in the world that have localized variations across different regions. For instance, you can find the American Yorkshire, the Australian Yorkshire, the Norwegian Yorkshire and the British Yorkshire. There are minor differences across these localized breeds.

The Yorkshire is characteristically white in color which strikes resemblance with the Poland China and the Chester White. It has erect ears. The breed cannot have black hairs on the coat as this makes it eligible for disqualification. However, small or indistinguishable amounts of black on the coat may be considered acceptable.

These are just some of the most popular pig breeds that you might be interested to try. There are several other pig breeds being reared for different purposes ranging from livestock needs to consumption requirements. Look for a breed that you can live with and manage. This helps you set realistic expectations from your associations.

2) Establishing a Genuine Source

Like every other animal you would like to take in as a pet, you need to be careful about where you purchase your pet pig. Establishing a genuine breeder should be one of your topmost concerns if you are hoping to have a long and healthy relationship with your pet.

Locating genuine and responsible breeders takes time and research. And even then, this does not necessarily mandate you will be able to find the breed of choice. So you need to be patient and consistent with your efforts in finding a breeder.

Keep in mind that the way your pet pig turns out, depends largely on the breeder. The general rule of thumb is that, a litter produced using healthy pigs will have a longer lifespan and be less prone to medical problems. In contrast, cross breeding or producing litter using diseased parents will result in the contrary. A breeder therefore is in control of the situation and needs to have ethical practices in order to promote longevity and healthy pigs.

Make sure you ask the breeder as many questions as you would like, even to the point of irritating the breeder. This ensures you are able to get the best deal. Put all your concerns to rest before you walk away with your pet pig in your hands.

The trickier part tends to be locating possible breeders within your vicinity. Seeing the nature of pig breeding in certain parts of the world, it might prove to be challenging just to locate a pig breeder, let alone a genuine or responsible one. So here are a few tips you can use on your hunt for pig breeders.

Firstly, look for links through the local pig clubs and associations. They will help you get in touch with the closest breeder. Because of their strict qualifying procedures, you can rest assured that the links will be authentic and the breeders you get in touch with will be responsible.

However, generally, such associations will not have an exhaustive network of pig breeders. So if you are unable to get the contacts you are looking for, you'll need to find your own contacts.

Search for pig breeders online. Try to locate livestock farming units within your vicinity that participate in pig rearing. The farms are a good place to purchase the pig from given you've ensured their breeding practices are in line with those set by local laws and pig breeding associations.

Make sure you visit them personally before having your pet shipped to your house. Better still, pick your pet from the farm yourself so you have a better idea of what it is accustomed to. This will help significantly down the line when you are helping your pet pig settle in your house.

If there is anyone you know who has acquired a pet pig, s/he will have a valuable lead for you to pursue. Get the details of the breeder and conduct your research to ensure it is a responsible one. Also, keep an eye on the development of this pig to see if it is prone to health problems or not.

Lastly, if you still haven't had much luck trying to locate the pig breeder, you can try searching local pet shops for some information. Although it is not recommended for you to purchase your pet pig from these shops – primarily because they don't share the intricate details about the parents and homing – it will nevertheless help you get started with your hunt.

Ask the pet shop owners about where they acquire their animals from and how they ensure the breeds are pedigree. Look for open and satisfactory answers. If they are not sharing important information about the pet acquiring process, it is better to look elsewhere. It is better not to have a pet than to settle for one which is prone to a number of behavioral and health problems.

Establishing a genuine source is therefore integral to a long term association with your pet. This is probably the longest part of your pet hunt. Make sure you read about the local rules and regulations pertaining to pet pigs as well. It is not always easy to keep a pig for a pet, especially where legal rules are extremely restrictive.

Make sure you ask the breeders for their registration papers with the local pig clubs. If they are unable to provide these, the next best thing you can ask for are medical certificates of both the parents used for the litter.

Pig breeding is an age old practice but it has conventionally focused on different reasons. As pet owners, you don't want a breed that accumulates more muscle and doesn't live beyond the first year! Choose the breeder wisely; it will help you a lot during the course of your companionship.

3) Meeting its Parents

Another important aspect of the pet acquiring process is meeting the litter's parents. Most genuine breeders will have them on the breeding grounds. Even if they don't, make sure you ask them for their pictures just to be sure that they are healthy and fit.

Pictures of the extended family are to be considered as a bonus because these aren't necessary. However, you need to ask as much as possible about the parents. This is because the genetics tend to replicate within the litter seamlessly. So even if the litter looks perfectly healthy during the initial months, they will be at risk of developing several health problems during the latter years if the parents had the same tendency.

Besides having a look at the parents, make sure you ask the breeder for their medical certificates as well. These documents declare the species clear of all major health problems and hence fit for mating. The absence of these records points towards an uncertainty with respect to your pet pig's health.

Another important thing that you need to verify is this; what was the age of the parents when they were allowed to mate? If the parents are too young – that is, within the first two years of their lives – then most genetic problems will not have surfaced by the time they were allowed to mate. In essence, medical certificates of pigs below two years of age do not have authenticity or value with respect to ethical breeding practices.

The first value lessons learnt by the litter are from their parents. Make sure you don't separate them before this value transmission is complete. This phase helps the pigs learn their characteristic habits (like rooting).

Cross breeding in pigs is not really considered as an illegal activity. But when this happens, you need to be extra careful about adopting the littermates. While cross breeding practices are adopted to improve the quality and life of a pig, most others end up in disasters. Especially if you are new to the task of keeping pigs as pets, it is recommended for you to pursue pedigree breeds only.

4) The Questions to Ask Yourself

There are a few questions that you need to ask yourself in order to gauge how serious you are about keeping pigs as pets. Never follow this pattern merely as a trend. Pet pigs are infinitely different from other animals. Make absolutely sure that you are looking for a pet pig before you decide to bring one in. If you can't live with the mess they are known to create, it is best to stay away from the association altogether!

Here is a list that might help you make the right decision. When you've answered these questions, evaluate them with a critical perspective. If, by the end of it, you still feel motivated enough to bring in a pet pig, then by all means you should proceed with the acquisition phase immediately!

1. Do you have the time and resources to care for a pet pig?
2. Do you really want to have a pet pig or are you just looking for a not-so-common pet for a companion? Have you evaluated other alternatives like birds, hamsters, turtles and others?
3. How much do you know about pigs' needs and breeds? Can you spot the differences between different pig breeds?
4. Do you have a lot of distractions that will make it difficult for you to care for a pet pig?
5. Do you travel a lot? If yes, how long do you think you will be away from the house? Can you take your pet pig on your trips?
6. Do you know how fast specific pig breeds tend to grow and how they will be when they mature? Some breeds grow faster

than others. On the other hand, some breeds are known for their small size!

7. Do you have access to a veterinarian doctor who will take a look at your pet pig if it is ill? It isn't a conventional pet so you might have trouble finding a doctor to consult if and when your pig gets ill.
8. Can you tolerate their natural habits like rooting? Do you have space in your backyard to accommodate their natural instincts? If these sound too dirty or disgusting, rest assured you won't be able to care for your pet pig in the right manner.
9. Can you keep up with a moody pet? Pigs get affected easily by the seasonal changes. They tend to become somber during winters and hyperactive during the summer season.
10. Can you accommodate a pet pig indoors? Pigs aren't outdoor pets. So you'll need to give them a space within your roomy interiors. But if you can't do so, it will affect your pig's health negatively.

Evaluate the pros and cons of your decisions carefully before you decide to bring a pig home. Because once you've adopted it, there is little chance you'll be able to get rid of the association responsibly before a decade or two!

5) The Questions to Ask the Breeder

Do you think you have what it takes to care for a pet pig? If you do, you would naturally want to move ahead with the acquiring phase. It is easy if you know where to go.

But if this is your first ever pet pig purchase and you have no one to guide you to a reputable breeder, you'll need to figure out the genuineness of the breeder by asking specific questions.

While at it, keep in mind that you have all the rights to get to know the breeder as well as the litter before you put down the payment, even if the breeder gets irritated by the questions!

A genuine and ethical breeder will never refrain from addressing your concerns. In fact, the authentic ones will ask you a couple of questions too in order to make sure you are the right owner for the pig!

Here's what you should definitely ask your breeder in order to identify how ethical s/he is in the breeding process.

1. How long have you been in the pig breeding business? The longer, the better!
2. How many generations of this particular breed have you witnessed? Are there any genetic complications I need to be worried about?
3. How frequently is the litter expected?
4. How are the littermates being housed? How are they cared for?
5. Were the parents certified to be health before they were allowed to mate?
6. What are the terms and conditions of the contract? What guarantees are present?
7. Are there any other clients you will be allowed to get in touch with in order to understand how the litter grows up to be?
8. How to take care of this breed? What to expect from pigs belonging to this breed?
9. How is the pig trained and socialized? Has the pig been taken to a veterinary doctor?
10. What all should I keep in mind while caring for this particular pig breed?

If there are any other questions on your mind, make sure you ask these! Clarifying your doubts need to be one of your top-most priorities.

If you feel the breeder has not been completely honest with you or if there are certain questions the breeder has tried to avoid at all times, you might want to consider looking elsewhere. If you are looking for a healthy relationship with your pet, you would be better off purchasing your pig from a breeder who is willing to share information with you!

In fact, professional breeders often look up to these questions as a sign of genuine interest. They encourage you to ask questions as it shows your eagerness to be the best owner for your pet.

6) The Questions to Expect From the Breeder

While you go about your routine trying to establish whether the breeder is authentic and ethical or not, the breeder will also want to make sure you are the right owner for their animals.

You can wholly expect them to ask personal questions. They will try to evaluate your resources and availability to keep a pig as a pet. The professional breeders are in no hurry to get their animals adopted, and they'll wait long enough for the right owner to find it!

They'll be interested in your lifestyle to see whether there is any space to accommodate a pet or not. This helps them ascertain that the pig will be well cared for and will therefore not end up on the street, euthanized or be brought back to the breeder.

Here are just some of the questions you should expect them to ask.

1. What work do you do for a living? This not only tells them how much spare time you have to care for your pet but also illustrates your financial situation.
2. Why do you want to keep pigs as pets? Do you have prior experience caring for pet pigs?
3. Where do you live?
4. Have you researched about keeping pigs as pets? What do you know about the breed and its caring needs?
5. Do you have any idea how much it costs to care for a pet pig?

There may be other similar questions about your personal life. All this while, the breeder will assess whether you can practically care for a pet pig or not.

So if, by the end of the day, the breeder decides not to give you a pig, you shouldn't despair. Instead, try to understand that the breeder has the best interests at heart – both for the pig as well as for you.

The questions here aim to give you an idea how you should analyze your needs for a pet. You should not fake answers just to have your way. Instead, be absolutely honest with the breeder – you might be able to find out a few facts you weren't considering before now. It can actually save you from a troubled relationship, if at all!

7) Picking the Right One from the Litter

If things go well during the question answer session, the breeder will introduce you to the pigs available on the farm at the moment. This is where you are required to select your companion.

Pigs, especially the younger ones, are absolutely adorable. Their little pink bodies and mischievous behavior will undoubtedly make you want to adopt them all.

However, it is generally a good idea to start with one pig to figure out if it is the right pet for you. Once you've understood your pet's needs, you can move forward with the second, third and the forth as you like!

Selecting a pig from the litter may prove to be a challenging task. A word of advice: don't make your choice simply based on how they look. You need to observe their behaviors in order to make the right selection. Their behaviors – even when they are little piglets – talk a lot about what they will grow up to be.

30

Here are some of the pointers which will help you make the right choice.

1. Look for a pig that likes being in the crowd. The one who lurks away in the corner while the others are playing is most likely to have certain personality disorders. The pig is unsocial from birth; it will take excessive training to make this particular pig social! In contrast with this, a pig that likes being in the crowd will most readily settle in with your lifestyle and will be happy around other pets!
2. A healthy pig will be active and playful. If there is any particular piglet in the litter that seems to be having some problems keeping up with the others, it is likely to develop more health problems in the near future. In fact if this is the case, we would recommend you not to purchase any piglet from the litter. This is a sure sign of trouble!
3. You definitely want to stay away from aggressive pigs. If any particular pig in the litter seems to be shoving others away without reason, this is the one you should avoid. They cannot only cause significant damage to your property and possessions but also pose a significant threat to people. Excessively timid pigs are to be seen critically as well. Pick a pig that seems to be on the moderate scale.
4. Check for the obvious signs of health. Their coats should be healthy and lively, their eyes should be bright and free from unexplained discharges, and there shouldn't be any stiffness or lameness in the way they walk. A healthy pig will be lively and interactive. They are fun and will therefore serve the purpose of a pet.

Keep your requirements in mind while picking up a pig from the litter. For the most part, you'll be looking for a well-behaved animal that will accompany you through the years without burdening you.

The piglet will exhibit most of the personality traits (if not all) that it is likely to have during its adult years. So if there are any particular aspects of the chosen piglet's behavior that you don't like, it is better to pick another one.

Be extremely careful about your choice. It is a matter of decades; you don't want to end up being stuck with a pig you cannot keep! Pay heed to the breeder's words and observe the piglets' activities closely. It will help you make a better choice!

8) Which Breed of Pigs is Best to Keep as Pets?

Not all pig breeds are the same. There are some breeds that are better as pets than others. When you are planning to buy a pig as pet, make sure you pick out the best breed. Below is some vital information on the best pig breeds to buy as pets.

Vietnamese Pot Bellied Pigs

This breed of pigs is very popular amongst people and is the most petted one. You must be wondering, why is this breed so desirable? Is it better than other pig breeds? Or is it more attractive?

Vietnamese Pot Bellied Pigs are further classified into three types known as; Lea, Royal, and Con.

The Lea pigs are very well-mannered and have a gentle appearance. They have a coat with black and white markings.

The Con pigs are bigger than Lea pigs. These pigs weigh 60-80kg. Their coat is black and wrinkled from the areas of face and head.

The Royal pigs are white in color and are larger in size.

Vietnamese Pot Bellied Pigs are categorized as exotic pets. These pets are bred and trained to live in homes so that they do not adapt to their natural-wild instincts. However, this is a misconception and a marketing tool that breeders use. A pig, no matter what breed, will never go against its instinctive nature. No matter how hard you try, your pig will adhere to its instincts. Pigs are wild animals. You can try and control its behavior, but you cannot change its nature. If you invest time to train your pig, it will become obedient and well-mannered.

Pennywell Pocket Pigs

Another famous pig breed is the Pennywell Pocket Pigs. This breed of pigs are very small in size. However, these pigs do not stay mini for their entire lives.

Pennywell is a farm in New Zealand, from where this breed got its name. These pigs can also be called micro-pigs because they are extremely small. Many celebrities have bought Pennywell Pocket Pigs due to their adorable looks. These cute pigs are easier to manage.

The Royal Dandie/ The Royal Dandie Extreme

A pig breed that is smaller than the Pennywell Pocket Pigs is the Royal Dandie. These pigs weigh 20 to 65 pounds and some rare ones are 20 to 35 pounds only. This breed of pig is a relatively new one and has been bred for 22 years only.

The Royal Dandie Pigs have beautiful colors and coat. Some are white, black, pink, and some have colored spots all over them. This breed of pigs is ideal for homes with kids. These pigs are extremely sociable, loyal, affectionate, and not to forget adorable. However, these pigs can be really expensive. The price of the Royal Dandie pig starts from $2000 in the US - £1320.

No matter which breed of pig you buy, you will need to make sure that you provide enough space for your pet friend. Pigs have exercising and grazing needs that need to be met or else they can become extremely challenging. If you live in an apartment or a home with limited space then a pig is not the right option for you. Pigs that are confined in small places and deprived of the outdoors tend to become destructive and extremely aggressive. Unless you are able to meet a pig's requirements, don't buy one.

Chapter 4: Some General Physical Characteristics

There are several pig breeds out there and each breed has certain distinguishing factors that differentiate one breed from another. Some pig breeds are quite popular for their size while some are known for their hyperactive nature. Despite these differences, there are quite a few similarities across breeds.

This chapter will try to address these similarities to help you understand how a pet pig differs from other pet animals. Those who have been rearing dogs will find pigs to be different. How different? Read through this section to get a realistic idea.

1) Their Origin

Pigs belong to the "Sus" genus of the "Suidae" family in the "Animalia" kingdom. Most pig breeds have become localized nowadays so that their origins are attached to the places they are commonly bred in. In fact, some breeds have adapted with the local climates. Hence most pig breeds are known to have originated from different countries across the world.

Theoretically, most pig breeds are known to have originated from the Eurasian and African continents. Over the years, these pig breeds were transported across the world for purpose of consumption as well as for pets. In different countries, this animal found different uses. The evolution of pigs reveals an exciting story.

Pigs are one of the most frequently cross-bred animals. They were constantly cross-bred for a number of reasons primarily revolving around quality improvement. Moreover, most of these cross-bred animals were localized into the environment, thereby creating different breeds with distinctive origins!

Depending on your geographical location, it is important to look out for a pig breed that has adapted well to these surroundings. This improves the chances of its survival and prolongs its life. So when you are hunting for a pet pig, make sure you've researched the local pig breeds well before making your selection.

2) Their Salient Physical Features

Biologically, a pig is quite similar to other mammals. However, it is in the appearance that they vary. Here are some of the salient physical features you will surely see across all pig breeds.

Firstly, and most evidently, the cylindrical snout is typical to this animal. All pigs are known to have a snout which helps them work with their rooting instincts. The snout is distinctively long which facilitates it in reaching the ground. The pig is known to have the sweat glands only on its snout. This is one of the main reasons the pig prefers being near mud or water to cool off their bodies.

Besides this, the pig is one of the rare animals that possess little or no neck. Their heads merge with their bodies seamlessly, seeming as though the animal does not have a neck. This can be attributed to the fact that most pig breeds have large heads which leaves little room to highlight the neck.

Also, pigs are known to have short legs. They are even-toed ungulates, that is, most pigs have even number of toes in their feet and that they are hoofed. This protects their tender toes from damages. It also helps them distribute their weight evenly across all points of contact with the ground. Hence the pig is capable of supporting hefty amounts of its own weight.

Their long triangular ears are also characteristic of this animal. In most breeds, the ears stretch over the eyes. In some, the ears remain outstretched.

Apart from this, another important fact about the pigs is this; their sense of smell and hearing is quite strong. However, most pig breeds do not have the capacity to see well. This explains why the pig is generally a slow animal despite being intelligent.

Lastly, pigs usually have a major part of their body mass accumulated on their lower body. This makes them ideal for consumption as the animal is capable of providing substantial amount of meat.

However, if you are looking forward to get a pig for a pet, you should be concerned about how you will accommodate it when it matures. Pigs can mature into a large animal weighing 400 to 600 lbs! This can be quite challenging to manage.

This is one reason small pig breeds are recommended for those starting out on their new-pet adventures.

Pigs usually have tough skins. However, they do not have the ability to sweat. They get sun burnt easily. This is why it is recommended to keep your pet pigs indoors and to use sun blocks and lotions on its body in order to prevent skin damage. Naturally, the pig keeps itself cool by covering its body with mud or water.

Some pig breeds may have hair while some others may not. Irrespective of this, pigs are known to have sensitive skin. So they need to be cared for especially as far as their skins are concerned.

3) Coat Colors

Different pig breeds have different coat colors. These range from white, black, brown to varying shades of red and pink. In fact, most white coat pigs actually appear slightly pink.

Most pigs have an undercoat of fine hairs. However, this does not provide them protection against the environmental conditions. This is one reason why it is important for you as the owner to take special care of your pet pig.

Besides this, healthy coats appear shiny and are free from wrinkles. They exhibit no dead skin cells and will usually flex perfectly over their vast bodies. You might want to keep this point in mind while picking up your companion. A healthy coat will most certainly point towards a healthy pig.

Some pig breeds have evident hairs while some do not. So you need to research a little about the pig breed that you are about to purchase. Even so, most pig breeds have fairly short hairs that appear bristly.

4) Height and Weight

The height and weight of the pig depends on the pig breed. Smaller pig breeds may be as small as about 13 inches high or may be as large as 5 feet high!

The largest pig ever documented in the history of this animal is a Poland China named Big Bill. It was about 5 feet high and over 9 feet in length. It is believed to have weighed over 2,522 lbs!

For starters, smaller pig breeds like the pot bellied pig and the guinea hog are ideal. These pigs stand about 12 inches tall and are well under 200 lbs weight. Hence they are easy to manage and accommodate.

Before deciding to purchase a pig, make sure you research well about what it becomes at maturity. Some pigs grow extremely fast into magnanimous creatures while some others don't grow much. The larger breeds may pose a challenge when they become full-grown.

5) Life Expectancy

The average life expectancy for most pig breeds ranges between 10 to 15 years. It is therefore advised to make a well-evaluated decision to acquire a pet pig. If you care well for your pet, you can even prolong its life by a couple of years!

6) Litter Size

On average, the pig litter amounts up to 12 piglets. It may be slightly different for specific pig breeds. Nevertheless, this gives you ample variety and choice to choose from.

However, the largest number of litter being noted for pigs is 37 piglets!

7) Personality

Pigs are popularly known for their social natures. They blend in well with people and other animals alike. This factor makes them particularly attractive for a pet. You can adopt a pet pig even if you already have other pets in your house; the pig mixes well with its surroundings.

In fact, for pigs, it is specifically recommended to adopt a pair instead of a single pig. This allows them to keep each other company, thereby putting lesser stress on you. As a general rule of thumb, however, you might want to start off with a single pet pig, bringing in the second companion at a later date.

Contrary to popular belief, pigs are actually clean and tidy animals. One would never see them relieving themselves near their food or sleeping area. Although rooting is a part of their natural instincts, they would rarely give you a reason to be upset.

As far as their individual personality traits are concerned, they can be extremely unpredictable. Some pigs tend to be amiable and charming while some others can be pretty notorious. Some wild ones may even prove to be nasty.

All pigs like being pampered. Some pigs would roll on their backs in order to get their tummy tickled. Some can be taught to jump and perform simple tricks. On the whole, pigs make remarkable companions and keep their owners delighted.

It will take some conditioning and training to allow the pig to settle in with the new surroundings. They usually learn well, so it is not like you need to keep badgering your pet pig day in and day out in order to make it obedient to your orders. If you make a clear and consistent statement a few times, it usually understands and retains well.

A major portion of their nature and personality comes from their initial value exchange phase. They learn their first few lessons from their litter mates as well as from the mother. A pig that has been separated prematurely from the mother or has been accustomed to the wild habitat will definitely pose difficulties in settling in to the home environment. This is why the breeder is of utmost importance when it comes to selecting your pet pig!

If you are planning to bring in an older pig, rest assured it will be an entirely different experience than brining in a piglet. An older pig will have distinctive personality traits that will be harder to change or influence.

8) Intelligence

Pigs are regarded as one of the most intelligent species that walk this planet. Some experts like to compare the intelligence of a pig with a three year old human baby. Pigs are capable of learning and replicating tasks with meticulous precision. Their intelligence is actually equivalent to a three year old baby!

Pigs are quick learners and will therefore grasp home rules quite easily. This also means that they will learn destructive tricks readily. For instance, pigs who learn to pull out the rug will continue to do so until and unless they are properly conditioned otherwise. Some pigs might even learn how to unlock the door, or get into cupboards. This may actually prove to be hazardous for the pig in the long run.

Like human kids, pigs like to put everything in their mouths. The first few weeks of their lives, the pigs will devour at almost everything that comes within reach of their mouths. For this reason, especial care needs to be taken while proofing the house for your pet pig. All small objects need to be removed from the floor and any other place that your pig will have access to.

Also, when they are out on a walk, it is recommended for you to use a full body leash to guide them. They will try to consume anything and everything that lies on the road. Anytime you feel there is something you shouldn't let it feast on, the full body leash will allow you to pick it conveniently.

Pigs are rapid learners and are therefore easily trainable. They will usually grasp house rules quite easily. Even if they don't, they can be easily taught to follow the rules by rewarding favorable behaviors. With their massive appetite, this method may prove to be the best kind of motivation.

On top of this, you can teach your pet to do simple tricks like jump or roll. You only need to work with them a few times to help them understand what is expected of them. Their learning periods are much shorter than those of dogs or cats. For the most part, your pet pig might not require any formal training sessions. You can figure out how to coach your pet pig by reading it out of a book! It is as simple as that!

Some people have taught their pet pigs to operate modern gadgets like computers as well. Pigs can replicate patterns with ease and hence may prove to be impressive artists. They can learn to manage simple appliances with ease. Although it is not always a good idea to give this kind of leverage to a pet pig, it is nevertheless entertaining for most people!

On the other end of the spectrum, pigs are known to have saved lives just like dogs and other pets! They are intelligent problem solvers and can therefore figure out a way out of trouble. Some distinguished pet pigs have performed wonders. They do not only sense pain and trouble but can call out for help when and if required.

Pigs are known to have a language of their own. They use different kinds of grunts and squeals to communicate their emotions. Most other animals can do little out of the ordinary.

Pigs are known to be natural swimmers as well. Despite their bulky bodies and small legs, they can swim across significant water bodies.

On the whole, pigs are regarded as an intelligent species, possibly more than dogs, cats or other pets of choice. They can learn to become smart or to become a menace. It largely depends on how you tackle the task!

Some pigs, if trained properly, may be disciplined to sense and understand emotions. You wouldn't need to use elaborate sentences or expressions to let the pig know you are upset with it. Their senses are strong, which helps them connect with their owners with ease!

9) Preferred Living Conditions

For the pigs, preferred living conditions involve an indoor setting but with access to the outdoors so that they can practice their rooting instincts. Since the pig cannot tolerate excessive heat or cold, it is recommended to keep it indoors. Use additional clothing during winters to keep warm. On the other hand, provide access to a mud or water pond during summers so that it can cool off!

Quite a few pig breeds have adapted to their local environmental conditions. It is a good idea to look out for these. Their adaption calls for minimal additional arrangements to accommodate seasonal changes.

It is important to keep in mind that the pig has extremely sensitive lungs. They can easily fall prey to pulmonary problems like pneumonia which may prove to be fatal for them. This is why the winter season may prove to be extremely crucial for your pet pig.

On the same note, it is important to keep in mind that seasonal changes can impact your pig's behavior. For instance, during the winter season, pigs tend to become withdrawn and depressed, less active and less interactive. The summer season makes them hyperactive and full of life! You need to keep these changes in mind while caring for a pet pig.

Apart from this, you need to remember that the pig likes to remain clean. While it loves coating itself in mud in order to cool off the summer heat, it will rarely do so with manure. Make sure you provide it with the right kind of materials to bathe in.

For pigs, the availability of an outdoor space involving loose soil is of utmost importance. Pigs cannot move away from their natural instincts. They need this space in order to root, that is, dig with their snouts. Unless you want them to destroy your garden space or your pots, you would rather give them their space to pursue their natural behaviors.

Pigs can make-do with a barn-like environment. Alternatively, you can train them to sleep in a bed. It is a good idea not to let them sleep with you in your bed because once they become habitual, it will be difficult to shake off their habits!

If, for any reason, you are unable to provide it with a mud spot inside or outside the house, you can alternatively provide it with a water pool. Most pig breeds tend to love the pool more than the mud. Given the choice, most of them would go for a swim in the pond rather than coat their bodies with mud. This further substantiates the fact that pigs like being clean.

Pigs generally live happily on farms – it is their natural habitat. They do fairly well in indoor environments as well. By and large, the pig is a highly flexible animal. It can be taught to adapt in any kind of an environment as long as its basic needs are being fulfilled. This is one reason why pigs make perfect pets!

10) Other Vital Statistics

At this point, you have a fair idea what to expect from your companionship with a pig. They are intelligent creatures that seem to have a mind of their own. At the same time, they like being pampered and will go any lengths to entertain their masters. They have a fair amount of natural skills that can amaze you.

The companionship of a pet pig is different by all means. So if you are heading out to purchase a pet pig, rest assured it will be a rewarding journey. While it is important for you to invest a major portion of your time selecting the breeder, here are some additional vital statistics that might help you gauge the health of your pick.

By rule of thumb, keep in mind that a healthy pig translates into a long companionship. Here's what you need to see in order to gauge the health of your pet pig.

- Temperature: about 39°C is considered normal for the pigs.
- Heart rate: it is 70-120 for pigs.
- Respiratory rate: a resting pig should have 32-58 breaths per minute. A pig at play will have a higher respiratory rate.
- Eyes: the eyes should be clear and bright, free from all kinds of unexplained discharges. Pigs can routinely accumulate dust in their eyes through play. Apart from this, no kind of discharge is to be considered normal.
- Coat: a shiny and clear coat is a sign of a healthy pig. Depending on the breed, you can look for the hair health as well. Nevertheless, if the pig has a fairly shiny coat beneath the hairs, it is to be considered as a healthy pig.
- Ears: for most pig breeds, their ears are placed on the top of their head slightly behind their eyes, either in an upright position or drooping over the eyes. They need to be pink and clean.
- Snout: the snout should be clear with no unexplained discharges.

- Musculoskeletal system: the pig should be able to walk properly. If it displays a limp or has difficulty walking straight, it is a sure sign of trouble. Also, it is in the nature of piglets to be curious and to experiment with everything. If a piglet fails to display this enthusiasm, it points towards an underlying problem.

Chapter 5: Temperament

Keeping pigs as pets means giving immense attention to them. Pigs love to be adored. They will roll over and enjoy long belly rubs. They will cuddle and they will mostly be hyperactive. If you are an affectionate person or you have experience petting dogs and cats, it'll be relatively easy for you to keep your pet pig happy.

Pigs have a combination of temperaments ranging from mild aggression to extremely affectionate. But for the most part, pigs are extremely playful and love excitement. They are curious creatures that are out to explore different things. Know the different temperaments of the pig before you pet one.

1) Is it Workaholic?

The pig is a hardworking animal and will learn different tricks. Keeping the pig is a great experience as it not only loves you back but it also works hard. Many people like to train their pets to learn certain tricks. The pig is one such animal that will exert its full potential to learn something. Pigs are not at all lazy and they will indulge in different activities which clearly prove that they do not run away from work.

Pigs love attention and can get bored easily, which means that keeping them busy in different activities is the way to make them happy. If you are having troubles with the temperament of your newly adopted pig, you can make it learn manners. Pigs are very similar to dogs and they will listen to their owners and stay obedient. Pigs are so hard working that they often run around the house trying to open cupboards and bins.

2) Behavior around Children

Pigs are extremely affectionate creatures that desperately need attention or they go under depression. Pigs are also very intelligent, mature and smart. That's why they can be left alone with children. It's like the pig can sense the innocence of kids and gets closer to them. They like to lie down, roll, and play with children. They are peaceful and act calm around kids. However, pot bellied pigs are said to be dominant over small children.

It is best to have kids and the pig together only when an adult is around. As stated earlier, pigs are like dogs. They tend to become dominant over the weak. Small children can be easy targets for pigs as they will try to get a hold of them. Another reason for having the pig and the kids under an adult's supervision is to avoid any encounter. Small children don't have control over their actions and can sometimes hurt pets. Their behavior can cause the pig to become aggressive. Otherwise, pigs go really well with children and show warmth and attachment.

When acquiring a pet pig, make sure you have talked to everyone in the house. Moreover, you will need to educate your family members about the behavior and temperament of pigs. There is no doubt that pigs are the most loving companions you will ever have but they do have their dark side. A pig's dark side i.e. its mood swings can become a tough thing to handle at first. However, when you start to get comfortable with your pet pig, it will not show its tantrums around you a lot.

Maintaining a safe environment within the house is very essential for pet pig owners. Pigs tend to get aggressive when they are bored or want food. The best thing to do is to not make them feel sad and provide them with enough food for the day. Another important thing to consider when you have a pig at home is to teach others to make it feel comfortable and not threatened.

3) Behavior around Other Pets

Pigs are social animals; that's why there is no doubt they will make friends with other pets in your home. Pigs make friends with cats and small dogs but they might not get along with big dogs. It is advised that you don't keep a pig and a dog together to avoid fights. It is always best to keep an eye on your pets, especially if you are leaving a pig with your dog.

4) Pigs around Cattle, Goats, and Sheep

If you have a farm where you have many sheep, goats, cattle, and pigs, you don't need to worry. Pigs don't feel threatened by livestock and will do absolutely okay around them. There are hardly any incidents between livestock and pigs. However, if you have a clever goat that likes to dominate, your pig will not do well with it. Apart from that, pigs and livestock animals don't cause trouble.

5) Pigs around Horses and Donkeys

Pigs and horses, donkeys, mules, etc, don't go too well together. Horses and animals under this category are strong and bigger in size. These animals often over-react that may cause mayhem. Horses and donkeys are also capable of hurting pigs, that's why it is not a good idea to keep them together.

6) Behavior around Other Pigs

Pigs love company but sometimes when you have a group of pigs living together, they might end up fighting every once in a while. Nature has created pigs in a hierarchy system but the levels are not clearly defined. Some pigs are dominant in nature while others are submissive. This means that the pigs that are dominant will try to boss around other pigs. This might result in a lot of fights, aggression, and behavior problems.

To ensure that the pigs stay safe together, you will need to train them to behave. This is the only way you can make the group work together or else you'll have to end up with a single pet pig. Of course all pigs are not the same. Every pig has a distinct personality and temperament. So, what dint work for someone else might work for you but is it a risk you would want to take or not is totally up to you.

7) Is It An Escape Artist?

Pigs are very clever and notorious that's why they are known to be escape artists. If you leave your pig outdoors without a fence, there's a high probability of it getting out of it. To keep them from escaping, install fences around your yard. Make sure the fences are not high above the ground because they will try to escape from underneath the fence. This escaping behavior is seen in pigs that are not satisfied with their living conditions. If your pig tries to escape every time you leave it outdoors, try to find out what it's missing. Provide your pig with a proper space, food, clean water, give your pig company and an area where it can take a dirt bath. The best way to avoid your naughty pig from escaping is by installing a good quality fence.

8) Pig's Natural Temperament

Although pigs are extremely affectionate pets, there are instances in which pigs have attacked their owners and other family members. So how does this happen? Why does a pig snap? Why does it get aggressive?

The temperament of a pig depends on a number of factors. The thing that most affects a pet pig is its living conditions. If you have created a perfect environment for your pet pig, there will be hardly any temperament issues. Pigs are non-violent if they are given proper care, food and companionship. They have some needs and when these needs are not fulfilled, a pet pig becomes aggressive.

It is natural for a pig to challenge others that it finds controllable. By nature pigs are very territorial. They would want to rule a place and when they see a threat or a more dominating personality, they will fight until they win. This is a behavior that pet pigs show to other pets and small children which they find easy targets.

The only thing that can stop this aggressive behavior in pigs is by training them. Training plays the most important role in making your pig a better pet. Without proper training, there will be no difference between a wild pig and your pet pig. If a pig is charging at you, you will need to adopt a strategy that will calm it in no time.

Pigs misbehave with the owners that pose themselves as weak in front of their pigs. When your pig gets aggressive and charges at you do not get scared. Pigs can sense your weakness and will begin to put you under pressure until it finally rules you out. You can stop your pig by grabbing the skin on its back and pushing it away with confidence. Do not over-do anything with your pig as it might worsen the aggression. Maintain a strong tone while scolding your pig but make sure it's not too loud.

9) Recognizing Aggressive Behavior in Pet Pigs

There are certain postures and actions that will identify that your pig is upset and will be charging at you or anyone near it shortly. Below are some distinctive signs that will tell you that your pig is angry.

- If your pig is swinging its head sideways.
- If your pig is snapping in the air.
- If it is biting on things.
- If it is jumping close to a pet, a child or anyone new, and then jumping away.

- If it is standing still with its head low.

10) Signs that Your Pig is Stressed or Afraid

Your pig will not react immediately to any threat, etc, but it will show its feelings with help of bodily postures, sounds and actions. A good owner will be observant of what its pig is doing. This will help the owner know about a pig's behavior before things go out of hand. Some of the common signs that point towards stressful and fearful behavior are:

- Chewing of the mouth with a white foamy discharge from the mouth.
- Starts to break things.
- Side swipe of the head quickly from the front.
- Twitching of the tail on one side.
- A long and heavy grunt.
- Charging at you or anyone else.
- Thinking and standing still.
- Tense body means that it is about to charge at you.
- Straight tail also means it is about to charge.

As pet pig owners, it is extremely essential to know what its body language means. This can help prevent fights, injuries and much more.

11) Pigs and Predators

Pigs are extremely social and love to make friends with other pets in the house. However, there are certain animals that should be kept away from pigs. In the wild, pigs are prey animals, which mean that they have a threat of becoming the meal of a predator. When pigs live with humans in their environment, their instinctive reactions don't change. Some pets in our homes can frighten our pigs, especially dogs. Pigs are not threatened by cats. However, dogs are predators and in the wild, they hunt pigs. That's why a pig is scared of a dog and might end up fighting with one if it feels threatened. When a pig makes a squealing sound, dogs may react fiercely and hurt them. It is not a good idea to leave your pigs with your dogs. Always supervise your pets when you give them time to socialize with your pig.

Another major concern for small pig owners is that they have many predators waiting to turn them into their meal. Piglets have a greater threat from many animals. Coyotes, eagles, falcons, etc are all enemies of a piglet. Never leave your baby pig in the open as birds will detect it and attack it.

12) Build a Solid Fence to Protect Your Pigs

If you have pigs in your home, make sure you have taken adequate steps to protect them from other animals, especially dogs. Build a fence or a solid enclosure for your pig so that it doesn't get attacked by dogs in the neighborhood. Get the highest quality fence for the boundary of your house. A strong fence will help protect your pig from dog attacks. Do not take your pig's safety lightly as dogs have the ability to tear down your pig and badly injure it. In worst cases, your pig might not survive the injuries, that's why it is extremely important to keep an eye on your pig and protect it from predator's eyes.

13) Types of Fences

Not every fence will be suitable for your pigs as pigs are extremely notorious when it comes to escaping. The size and the material of the fence plays a vital role in keeping your pigs from escaping, especially the little ones that easily escape from under the fence. When choosing a fence for your pigs, you have to keep in mind that it is meant for two purposes, i.e. to keep them from escaping and to protect them from predators. Pigs do not jump off the fence; they sneak from under it or break through it. A fence that is fixed deep in the ground serves to be the best.

Many people opt for electric strand fencing which is extremely helpful in keeping male and female pigs separated from each other. This is usually the case when the pigs are un-neutered or un-spayed. Moreover, such a scenario is common in farms where pigs are bred and not in homes.

Wooden Fences

When you have several pigs in an enclosure or a backyard, you need to have strong fences. Wooden fences are feasible for pig. However, the wood shouldn't be weak as pigs can easily break through it. Pigs have sharp teeth and a lot of power. They can easily break and destroy poor quality wooden fences. Wooden fences will turn out to be effective only if the material is strong and thick. Install the wooden fence tightly into the ground or else it will be very easy for your pigs to escape.

Wired Netting

Wired or metal netting is the most common type of fencing used for pigs. Unlike wood, wired fencing is not easy to destroy. Many farmers and breeders use sharp wired fencing to keep pigs in one place or separated from other animals. Netting however, isn't sharp but is made in a way that it doesn't provide free space to pigs which helps in keeping them from escaping.

Although there are numerous benefits of wired netting, it may be harmful for piglets or small breed pigs. Small pigs tend to get stuck in little spaces of the net and injure themselves. To provide better protection, insert the wire into a concrete floor so that the pigs cannot dig the ground.

14) Signs that Your Pet Pig is Feeling Relaxed

There is a lot of discussion on the aggressive temper of pigs. However, pigs usually stay in a fun mode. Pigs are just like dogs; they love to play, cuddle and give company to their owners. Giving endless love, food, treats, and entertainment to your pigs will keep it happy and content. There will be hardly any incidents that your pet pig will charge at you or bite you. A greater part of a pig's behavior depends upon the kind of training it got from its owner.

Pigs do not get aggressive all the time. There are certain actions, sounds and postures that pigs show when they are happy and relaxed in your home's environment.

- If your pig shuts its eyes.
- If your pig flops on sides.
- If it rubs itself on your legs.
- If it sniffs the floor.
- If it is grinding its teeth.
- If it holds the snout in the air to explore.
- If it is wagging its tail like a dog.

Do look out for your pig's relaxed expressions and note the things that make it feel comfortable. This will help you give a better idea of what your pig really likes and you can do more of those things.

15) Things You Should Take Care of!

There are other factors that contribute towards a bad behavior in pet pigs that usually stay calm and happy. Below are some reasons that can make your pet pig aggressive and out of control.

- If your pig is used to being around people all the time, do not leave it alone at home. Many owners make this mistake and end up making their pig aggressive forever. Pigs are affectionate animals, but at the same time they are sensitive and overly emotional. Once they get attached to someone or get used to an environment, they will not accept any changes. So, when your entire family wants to head out, make sure you take your pet pig along OR if you cannot do that, leave at least one person back at home. This also happens because a pig feels lonely without people around it. When it doesn't get the company it wants, it becomes angry and starts to act up with its owners as well.
- If you have always fed a lot of food to your pet pig, it will become really hard to cut down on it. That's why new pig owners are advised to not over-feed their pigs. Keep your pet pigs at 2 bowls per day. More than that means obesity and bad

health for your pig. When overweight pigs develop health problems, vets advise to limit their diet. In this situation, majority of pet pigs don't take it too well as they are used to eating a lot of food.

- Excessive treats have always become a major problem for pig owners. During the training process of pigs, many owners offer a lot of treats to their pigs so that they learn quickly. However, by giving excessive treats to their pigs, owners are actually making them feel that it is easy to get a treat. This is not the right approach for training a pet pig as it will follow your rules once and after getting a treat it will forget what has been taught. So, when you stop offering treats to your pig, it will get aggressive and chew on things.

- Leaving pet pigs alone with other pet animals becomes a great problem as pigs are territorial. When you leave your pigs alone with your dog, they will get into a fight. These fights happen because dogs and pigs are both territorial animals. They both are bossy and will fight if they feel threatened. That's why do not make a mistake of leaving your pigs with other pets. Always keep them together under your supervision.

Chapter 6: Evaluating the Pros and Cons

The history of pigs and humans date back to a thousand years and that's why they are called exotic pets. Pigs are extremely social and intelligent. Their nature is what makes them so desirable amongst humans and many of them keep them as pets. Pigs are friendly animals and they keep themselves very clean. There were times when pigs were misunderstood to be unhygienic and no one kept them as pets. Since the rise of animal welfare and awareness programs, people got to know the real side of pigs i.e. a friendly and fun loving companions.

1) The Good Part about Pigs as Pets

Pigs have a lot of pros as they are animals that yearn for human attention. They are extremely sensitive and want to spread love. When you keep pigs as a pet, you will need to give it proper company. Pigs get depressed very easily which means that you need to take out time for them and keep them happy. They would roll over for a tummy rub or would want to snuggle with you. They are loving and loyal as a dog.

Another great trait of pigs is that they are very clever and intelligent. Pigs have a sharp mind and memory. They will learn tricks pretty fast, that's why pig owners should teach them different tricks. They also obey commands from their owners. A pig's brain is so good that it is proved to be one of the best amongst other animals.

Pigs are excellent communicators. They love to express their feeling with the help of different sounds. A pig will squeal, bark, cry, cough and laugh. If your pig is feeling happy, it will make a squealing sound which sounds like a laugh. This indicated that your pig is excited. Pigs bark when they feel threatened. If you do not accompany your pig, you might hear a deep cough sound, which means that your pig is upset or angry. Pigs make cough sounds when they are feeling lonely or they don't get food.

Pigs are excellent sniffers. They can smell anything 25 ft under the ground. They are very curious animals and will use their smelling power and memory to recognize things. If you have food near them, they are probably going to sniff it out.

Pigs are perfect for people that catch allergies from pets. They don't need a lot of maintenance because they don't shed a lot. Pigs are conscious creatures that like to stay clean and hygienic. They do not like dirt on them and don't mess-up your home. They are odorless and will keep themselves super clean, which makes them the best pets to have.

2) The Concerns over Pig as Pets

Pigs are harmless animals but they have some qualities that some people might find unattractive.

Pigs can become very messy sometimes when they do not get adequate attention from their owners. We have constantly discussed about a pig's friendly and loving nature. This means that they do not want to be left alone. Lonely and bored pigs often get destructive. They will eat dry wall, dig up the ground, ruin your carpet and flooring and turn over trash cans. Pigs show this destructive behavior usually when they are hungry and in search of food. If you are planning on keeping a pig as pet, make sure you give it undivided attention and lots of food.

Pigs have a natural habit of rooting in dirt and soil to find food. Rooting can turn out to be very messy. Do not leave your pet hungry because it will destroy everything in a very harmless way.

Pigs are not messy animals if you provide them with proper attention and desired space. Happy pigs are the best pets. If your pig doesn't get what it needs, however, then it will find a way to get it on its own. In hot days of summer, pigs will need a cool environment because their body temperature rises. If you will not provide them with a cool environment, it will dig deep into mud or jump in water. It is best to provide your pet pig with a little pool of its own so that it stays happy and cool.

A pig's lungs are very sensitive and their size is small. That's why they need to be protected from the changing weather. Pigs are prone to catching lung diseases and infections. A pig can die from pneumonia or other weather sickness.

Pigs are intelligent animals and they learn different tricks quickly. The pig's main motivation is food and it will do anything to get it. A mischievous pig will open cabinets, fridge, doors and bring down trash cans in search of food. They need to be under the supervision of their owner or they'll play tricks. But all of these habits of a pig can be changed if it is given proper attention, care, love, and food.

Chapter 7: The Acquisition Process

A proper adoption shelter usually conducts a detailed evaluation of anyone that wants to adopt a pig. A typical pig acquisition process includes applying for adoption, home evaluation, discussion on concerns, meeting the pigs, final process, and adoption fee. Shelters ensure that the pigs go into right families and introduce them to new families before handing them over so that their behavior could be evaluated. A pig's price may vary from country to country.

Important: please note I didn't buy pigs from the websites mentioned here. Make sure that you check out the breeder/seller thoroughly before you buy.

1) Where to Buy a Pig in the US?

Animal adoption centers are at large throughout the US and that's why it is not that hard to find a pet pig for yourself. If you are having troubles locating a pig adoption center, simply search the Internet. Many adoption centers have their online websites for the convenience of people. To find a pet pig for adoption on the Internet, read on to the list of links given below.

- http://www.adoptapet.com
- http://www.pigs4ever.com
- http://www.teacuppigsforsale.org
- http://www.texastinypigs.com
- http://www.royaldandie.com
- http://www.vegaspigpets.org
- http://www.whenpigsflynaked.com

2) Where to Buy a Pig in the UK?

Just like the US, pigs in the UK are also adopted or bought from pet shops and adoption centers. Some pigs can also be bought from breeders. People in the UK can find a pet shop on the internet and contact it to buy or adopt a pig. Below is a list of pet shops and adoption centers in the UK that you can surf on the internet for more details.

- http://www.valleyofthepigs.co.uk
- http://www.preloved.co.uk
- http://lancashiremicropigs.co.uk
- http://kewlittlepigs.com
- http://www.freerangepigsireland.com

You can buy a great book about Micro Pigs here: www.micropigshed.com

3) Estimated Prices for this Pet

Pigs have gained popularity and many people are willing to keep them as pets. There are different breeds of pigs available on the market and every breed comes with a different price tag. Some pigs are more expensive than others, especially teacup pigs. A pig's price ranges depending on your location. In the US, you can buy a pig for as low as $40 - £26 or as high as $1500 To $2000, £990 to £1320. Some pigs can be adopted without a price as well. In the UK, pigs can be bought at a price ranging from £0 to £700. Miniature breeds of pet pigs are sold at higher prices all around the world.

4) Signs of a Healthy Pig

A healthy pig will simply look healthy and be easy to identify. If you are still confused, however, there are many other signs that will tell you about its health. When you are at a pet store or breeder to buy a pig, you will need to keep your eyes and mind open. Observing the environment the pig lives in will help you know the pig a little better. Never buy pigs from a breeder that doesn't take care of the pig's hygiene, its nutrition, its health, and its physical needs. The pigs that are handled in a poor way become aggressive, depressed, snappy, and much more.

Therefore, it is extremely important for owners to ensure that the pig that they are buying is in perfect shape. If you don't be careful in buying a healthy pig, you'll end up spending a lot of money on its healthcare, grooming, training, etc.

Its Records

To identify whether a pig is healthy or in poor shape, one can look up in its history. For people that want to adopt pigs as pets, ask for its records. Any adoption center, pet shop, or breeder usually has a file of documents that tells about the medical history of the animal. In those records you will find out about its vaccinations, health, age, and many other factors that will point out whether the pig you are interested in is healthy or not.

It is better to read through different articles and do your research prior to visiting a pet shop. If you are interested in buying a female pig, look up its records to check its age. Then find out whether that pig had babies or not. This way you will get insight on the pig and its health conditions. Apart from records, you can also observe the pig from a distance. Note things that you find unusual about it. Some pigs might seem more hyper than others while some will look depressed. These are all signs that will help you in your buying decision and will help you get a perfectly healthy pig as a pet.

Some Physical Indicators

To know more about a pig's health before you buy it depends greatly on its physical characteristics. When you visit a pet shop to get a pig, stand at a far distance and observe the animal. Observation will tell you a lot of things about a pig's health. If the pig seems in poor condition, slow or sick, you will get to know by just looking at it for a few minutes. Below are some questions that will be answered after observing a pig you are interested in.

- Is the pig eating, walking, and acting properly?
- Is the pig slow? (pigs usually remain excited, this means that a slow and dull pig has some problems)

- Does it have bruises and wounds?
- Does it have abnormal swelling in any part of the body?
- Does the pig look clean?
- Is there a sick pig in the same enclosure containing healthy pigs?
- Is the pig the right size?
- Is the pig thin or fat?
- Is the pig shedding hair?
- Does it have a lot of fur?
- Is the pig's skin fine or does it have lumps, sores, spots, scratches, etc?
- Does the pig look hygienic?
- Does the pig have lice, fleas or parasites?
- Does it discharge abnormally from the mouth or the snout?
- Does the pig's breath smell bad?
- Does it have blood marks on the skin or any part of the body?
- What is the color of the inside of its eyelids?
- Is the pig coughing?
- Is it breathing normally?
- Is the pig's penis, testicles and vulva in perfect shape?
- Do the pig's joints look abnormal or is there any swelling?
- Are the pig's feet clean?

5) The Registration

Once you have bought a pig for yourself, you will need to go through its registration process. Every country has different laws, which is why one needs to agree to follow the rules and only then get confirmation from the government to keep the pet.

According to the UK law, if you are keeping a pig as a pet, you will need to register it with Animal Health and Veterinary Laboratories Agency (AHVLA). This agency will register your pet pig to protect the people and the pet from threats and different circumstances. Other agencies that work with it to help support pet pigs include; Parliamentary Under Secretary of State for Resource Management, the Local Environment and

Environmental Science, Animal Health and Welfare Board for England and Animal and Plant Health Agency. The UK government wants to ensure that a pet pig is getting proper food, living environment and care based on their needs. Animal welfare agencies also advise pet pig owners to take proper care of them. To register your pig you can call your Animal Health Office and they will provide you with a herd's mark for your pig or pigs. Your pet pig's registration will be confirmed when you will receive a letter of confirmation from the AVHLA.

For pet pig owners in the US, you have to get your pig registered as soon as you bring it to your property. For people's convenience, some websites help you register online; http://www.americankunekunepigsociety.com

American Kune Kune Pig Society also registers pet pigs. This society registers those pigs that are tagged as non-breeding pigs. The American Pet Pig Association is another agency that allows owners to register their pet pigs. They also provide information and awareness on pigs to their owners. Their site http://www.americanpetpigassociation.com also provides information on pig breeds that can be kept as pets. You can fill out their registration form and register your pet pig at http://www.americanpetpigassociation.com

6) Decisions to Buy

So, you got your eyes on a pretty pig but fall into confusion. You want to be sure that your buying decision is right. Unless you have done your research, you will need to keep certain things in mind before confirming the pig. The most important thing that one needs to keep in mind before buying the pig is to check its parents. Many breeders breed diseased pigs and their diseases are inherited by their piglets. This is a major problem that most pig owners complain about.

Make sure you visit the breeding place and living area of the pig. This will give you an idea about the pig's lifestyle and its behavior. Pigs that are kept in confined spaces in breeding farms are often ill-mannered and aggressive. These pigs do not get proper environments which makes them depressed or go under massive stress. Training such pigs can be a tricky job and if you are not up for it, make sure you investigate before buying the pig.

One, Two, or More

When buying a pig as pet, make sure you have chosen the right breed. Some pigs can grow really fast and can weigh up to 200kg. These huge pigs can cause a lot of trouble at homes and run around breaking household items, fences and digging up the ground. Small sized pigs are less tricky to handle and are easy to manage. Pigs get bored really soon and need constant attention and companionship. If you know you cannot give them company throughout the day, pet two pigs. A lonely pig can become very destructive and easily gets depressed. Moreover, how many pigs to pet entirely depends on your capability to handle them. However, make sure you are not keeping non castrated male with a female. If you are interested in petting more than one pig, make sure you have a proper enclosure for them.

Male or a Female

A female pig makes a better pet than a male pig. Male pigs are also great pets but they should be castrated. A male pig that is not castrated can become aggressive and have frequent mood swings. If you are buying a pair, make sure both the pigs are neutered and spayed or else they will create a lot of trouble.

The Best Age

There is no age restriction in pigs. However, it is suggested that people buy younger pigs. Old pigs are prone to getting sick and are huge in size. Either get a piglet or a younger aged pig as a pet.

Chapter 8: Preparing to Bring Your Pig Pet Home

When you are bringing your pet pig home, you need to make sure that it is comfortable around you. Scared pigs can react in different ways that's why it is extremely essential for you and the pig that you are familiar with each other. Transport your pig with help of a pet carrier or a sky kennel because it is the safest for you and the pig. Before the pig's arrival, make sure its new home is all set to welcome it. Pigs are loving animals and they need certain things in their surroundings to make them feel comfortable, relaxed, and happy. Angry and scared pigs can become a trouble that's why it is important to transform your pig's new home into its dream home.

1) Proofing Your Home

Before you bring your pet pig home, make sure that the indoor environment of your home is suitable for it. Moreover, you will need to follow certain precautions to protect yourself and home from a new member of the family. If you have chosen a smaller breed of pig, make sure your house is safe for it. Take care of the surroundings as a teacup pig is just like a little toddler not knowing what's good or bad. You will need to remove any sharp, pointy, and slippery objects from your home. Your house should be hazard proof so that the pig can roam around freely without any harm. Pigs are curious animals and they will eat anything, that's why it is important to keep away food items from its reach. Apart from food items, pigs eat anything they find on the ground including rubber bands, small toys, etc. So don't leave any objects unattended on the floor or near your pet pig.

Another thing you must take care of is your bins. Pigs are naturally curious and will try to destroy your bins in search of food. Try to keep your bins and garbage cans away from your pig's reach or just shut them tightly so that your pig doesn't sabotage it. Do not leave your deodorants, creams, and hazardous objects near your pig, as it is capable of hurting itself and destroying your home. Pigs love to escape, that's why it is important to create a strong fence outside your yard or garden. Don't leave doors open as they will try to escape and you'll find them running outside. Keeping pigs as pets means responsibility. You cannot neglect them and keeping an eye on them is very important.

Pigs love dirt and mud. As an owner, you should take care of their needs. Keep a pool of dirt for them or they'll start digging up your garden. If you have adopted a young pig, make sure you are extra cautious with it. Little pigs are fragile but can be very cunning at the same time. The way your pet pig behaves entirely depends on its training. When you get a pet pig, give it proper training so that it doesn't get destructive and act obediently.

2) Inspecting the Extent of Proofing

Your home's proofing should be done perfectly before your pet pig arrives. Pigs need a lot of care and attention. You cannot neglect them especially if they are not trained or young. It is good to create a separate space for your new pet pig. You will need to check your entire home and proof it from any hazardous substances or objects. Small furniture items, stools, and chairs can also be dangerous for your pig. Make sure you don't have a lot of little objects everywhere in your house. Remove hazards like fire, flame, chemicals, choking, falling, etc. Inspect your home thoroughly and then welcome your new pig home. Pigs have hard feet that can easily slip on slippery floors or marbles. Before bringing your new pig home, make sure you have covered your stairs and other areas with carpet.

3) Preliminary Shopping List for Your Newfound Pet

You will need to go out for shopping before your pet joins the family. There are certain things that a pig requires and to ensure that your new family member stays happy, you will need to buy a list of things.

- **Treats** – Pigs are very similar to dogs that love to eat treats. Your new pet pig will need lots of training. In the training process, you will need to give it treats as a sign of appreciation. Pig treats are available on pet stores, online stores and your local store as well. Buy peanut butter biscuits for your pig as treat. As there will be a lot of training in the initial days, buying treats is a must.
- **Pig Food** – Pigs love to eat, that's why make sure you have bought a lot of food for them in advance. You can get reviews on different pig food on the Internet or from your local pet shop.
- **Pig Couture** – If you have bought a pig in the winter season, make sure you have bought warm clothes for it. Pigs like to roam outdoors and can catch cold. To keep them warm you should buy soft and comfy coats for them.
- **Harnesses** – Your pig will need a harness when you take it for a walk or leave it in the open. Harnesses are easily available at pet stores, big stores, and the pet shop you got your pig from.
- **Health Care** – Your pig will need extra care. You will need to buy insect repellents, shampoo, first aid kit, etc for your pet pig to maintain its oral health and hygiene.
- **Grooming** – Grooming is an essential part of your pig's healthcare. Get shampoos, creams, hair brush, and hoof trimmers for you pig to maintain its hygiene.
- **Feeding Pans** – Get feeding pans made out of stainless steel for your new pet pig.
- **Poop Cleaner** – You will need to get a pooper scooper for your pig to easily clean the floor or ground.
- **Toys** – Pigs love to play and have little fun. That's why you will need to buy toys for their entertainment. Buy ribbons, leash, plastic or rubber balls with food, cardboard, wooden box, sandboxes, paper balls, etc. These things are really important for pigs or else they will try to find things to play in your house.

Chapter 9: The Initial Days

For some people the initial days of getting a pet pig home are very difficult. However, this discomfort can be avoided by getting knowledge about pigs from your pet shop or the Internet. Pigs are the 5th most intelligent animals and understand their owner's commands very well. When your pig has arrived, make sure you make it feel comfortable. Below are some points that will help you get along with your new pet pig.

1) The First Few Days and Weeks

Pigs are affectionate animals and crave love from their owners. When you have bought a pig and bring it home, its initial days in your home are going to be a little challenging for you and the pig itself. Just like humans take time to settle and get familiar with a new place, pigs also need a few days to relax in a new home. Their behavior entirely depends on the way you treat them.

Pigs usually stay in a happy mood. However, there are certain factors that are responsible for their good mood including the place they live in. as owners, you will need to create a happy environment for your pet pig. Keep a comfy bed for your pig with a blanket. Pigs love to sleep in soft and warm blankets. They will gel with you in no time if you have provided your pig with a mud pool, water pool, and lots of food.

It doesn't take a lot of days for a pig to get comfortable in a new environment because they are loving animals. All they need is love from their owners. Pigs are social animals and always want someone around them to give them company. During the first few weeks, you will need to provide them a lot of attention, love, and cuddles.

In the initial days, you will also need to get used to your pig's behavior, feeding time, and poo time. Observe with an open mind and note your pig's timing. You can also train your new pet pig as it is a clever animal and picks up new tricks in no time.

Pigs need a lot of physical exercise to stay fit and healthy. Make sure you do not restrict your pig to indoors only. Take your pig on a walk in the morning time. Pigs are most active after a good nap. That's why give them time in the morning just after they wake up. If your pig will find itself alone at anytime, it will start to destroy things and get aggressive. It is advised that owners accompany their pigs and avoid leaving them alone.

2) Setting the Rules

Pigs are mischievous and curious by nature. They will run around your home in search of entertainment or a good time pass. Your pig will also need ample training before it becomes obedient. Pigs are smart and they learn pick up things pretty fast.

Your new pet pig won't know when it's enough. There will be times when you will find your pig in the garbage can or running around the house with a toilet roll in its mouth. Pigs can become destructive and messy if they are trained to listen to orders. As owners you will need to set some rules and make the pig follow them. A pig's brain works very well. If your pig is doing something it shouldn't, try to stop it by saying 'NO' in a strong voice. The pig will take a few days to learn what's wrong and what's right. Remember, you cannot force a pig to follow the rules. Adopt a positive reinforcement strategy to make your pig obey you or else it will get aggressive.

Pigs have a dominant nature as they are categorized by nature as prey animals. They don't like to be bossed around. Make sure you are not threatening your pet pig and make it follow the rules in a polite tone. Pigs will need to be toilet trained in their initial days in a new home. Place a litter box near the pig containing soil, so that the pig gets used to it.

3) Common Mistakes to Avoid

When you have bought a pig as a pet, you will need to avoid certain mistakes.

- Keep a record of your pig's vaccinations, medical files, and medical history.
- Do not leave your pigs alone with toddlers because some pigs will try to dominate them.
- Don't put your dogs and pigs together.
- Don't leave your pigs unattended in the outdoors.
- Do not over or under feed your pig.
- Do not leave hazardous items around your pig.
- Get rid of sharp objects.
- Get rid of slippery floors to avoid hurting your pig.
- Do not leave your hand in pig feed for a long time as pigs are omnivores, they will chew anything that comes in their mouth.
- Do not feed plain dry food all the time as it can cause choking and swallowing problems.
- Pigs with pink skin are prone to sunburns and dry patches. Do not leave them under the sun for too long.
- Do not forget to trim your pig's hooves.

4) *Ways to Bond with Your Pet Pig*

Pigs are affectionate and friendly by nature, that's why it is not too hard to bond with them. With a little effort, a pig will start to consider you its friend. Your new pet pig would want to stay close to you and will love some cuddling in the bed. Make a mini bed for your pig and place it near your bed. This will give your pig a feeling of comfort and safety. Pigs also love to play and have fun, that's why they will enjoy being with an owner that plays with it.

Another way to bond with your new pet pig is to offer it food. You can sit on the floor near your pig and offer it food. Pigs love to eat and they will accept your offer of friendship when you will give them lots of food to eat.

Give gentle scratches to your pig on its chin or back. Pigs are like cats and dogs; they will love to be scratched and will feel more comfortable around people that create a physical bond with them.

Positive reinforcement also helps keep your new pig comfortable. You should adopt a polite tone while talking to your pig or during its training. This will make the pig feel good and it will bring it closer to you.

If you live with your family, make sure you make your pig used to everybody. Pigs will not like unknown faces and might react to them differently. To maintain a happy and healthy environment at home, you must familiarize all the house members with your pig.

Sometimes pigs need time to settle and make them comfortable around new faces. That's why many pigs don't react well to too much attention and touching. If your pig is irritated when you pick it up or give it a rub then maintain your distance. The worst thing you could do to make your pig feel uncomfortable and afraid is by following it when it runs or hides. Touch your pig gently and reach for him from below. If you will try to touch or pick it from above, it will feel threatened and will make squealing sounds.

Overall, pigs are extremely love animals and they love getting attention from people. The initial days are going to be a little tough but your pig is most likely to react well to all that attention.

Bonding with your pet pig doesn't mean you can let it do whatever it desires. Maintain rules throughout the bonding process or else your pig is going to adopt those habits which will turn out to be annoying in the later days.

Chapter 10: Caring for Your Pet Pig

Pigs are great pets and they'll fit in perfectly if you train them to follow your house rules. Setting rules will not only keep your pig safe but it will also be good for other family members and your home. When you bring your pig home, you will need to ensure that your home's environment is perfect for the pig. You will also need to make sure that the place is safe for the pig. Apart from the basic considerations, you will need to manage all the things accordingly.

1) Its Grooming Concerns

Pigs are hygienic animals and do not like getting messy. That's a plus point for pig owners as they don't need much effort to keep it clean. However, there are certain grooming concerns that every pig owner should keep in mind. Pigs do not have fur but they definitely need some grooming to stay in perfect shape and stay absolutely adorable.

The Ears

Pig's ears gather a lot of earwax and that's why you will need to clean its ears on a frequent basis. Use a damp cloth or Q-tips to get rid of the wax. Be cautious while using Q-tips as it can hurt your pig.

The Eyes

Pigs often develop crud around or under their eyes. Curd makes the eyes and face look dirty that's why it is important to check your pig's eyes and clean them. You can take a damp piece of cloth to remove it gently using your hands.

The Skin

Pig's skin gets sun burnt easily and becomes dry and irritating. Buy a lotion for your pig and apply to its skin if it gets dry or damaged. A lotion can also be applied after a bath. This will keep your pig's skin soft and protected.

The Hooves

Hooves grow pretty fast, that's why they need trimming or filing. You can file your pig's hooves regularly to avoid the hassle of getting them trimmed.

The Tusk (in males)

If you have a neutered pig, its tusk will not grow but if it is not then you will need to trim them. If you observe a rapid growth in your pig's tusks, visit your vet and set an appointment. Trimming of tusks can only be done by vets as it requires anesthesia.

Brushing

You can brush your pig while giving it a bath. Use the brush gently on your pig's skin as it can get irritated easily.

Bathing

Pigs are clean animals and they don't require a lot of bathing. That's why bathe it only if it has dirt on it or the skin is getting dry. Buy a pig shampoo from a store and give your pig a bath with your garden hose. Only use tepid water when bathing your pig. Extreme temperature water can be harmful for your pig.

2) Feeding Concerns

One thing is certain: pigs love to eat. Your pet pig will need a lot of food and if it doesn't get enough, it will start digging up dumpsters and damaging your property. A happy pig is the one that gets lots of food and treats. Your pig requires a balanced diet of fruits, vegetables, and proteins. Make sure you give your pet pig lots of fiber in the form of hay, bran, etc.

What to Feed Your Pig?

Your pig's main source of food will come from pig food that you can get from the market. Pig foods are packed with nutrition, proteins, and energy for your pig. Your pig would want food all the time but it is in your hands to keep a control over it. Pigs require a fiber rich diet that's why it is important to let them graze in your garden or yard. A diet containing 14 to 15% protein is suitable for a pig.

Feeding Young Pigs

Little piglets should be fed 3 to 4 times a day, as they cannot consume a lot at one time. Your little pigs will need to be fed milk with help of a feeder. Your pig will try to break the feeder but once it gets used to it, you shall have no problems feeding with it. You can also buy a cereal for your piglet and mix it in the milk. This will provide your pig with proper nutrition.

Feeding Adult Pigs

Adult pigs will need a diet packed with nutrition. You can feed them 2 ½ cups of pig food from the pet store in one time. You can feed them fruit scraps, vegetables, and bread. Your adult pig might feel hungry several times in a day but don't over feed it. Train it to eat food two times a day.

Frequency of Feeding

Just because pigs like to eat a lot it doesn't mean you can over feed your pig. Over feeding your pig can cause a number of health and weight problems. Over-weight pigs suffer from disability; and in worst cases, they might die. Treats should also be kept on a low, as giving too many treats will make your pig greedy and not to forget fat. Little ones will need to be fed several times a day.

Some Healthy Treats for Pigs

Pigs will need treats as they will be in a constant training process. Pig treats can be made at home or bought from the store. Treats mean little quantity, even a single salad leaf would do. So, avoid giving too many treats, as it will ruin your pig's habits and diet. The treats that you can give your pig are:

- Grains
- Bread
- Vegetables
- Fruits
- Peanut butter and popcorn

Some Potentially Harmful Treats for Pigs

Do not give leftovers or food rich in sugar, salt, or protein to your pigs. Your pig will happily accept any food item you offer, but as the owner, it is your job to know what can harm your pig's health and what can be healthy for it. Meat, poultry, pretzels, potato chips, cakes, fish, chocolate, canned foods are treats that shouldn't be given to pet pigs. Some foods should be fed in a limited quantity including potatoes, tomatoes, corn, fruits high in fructose, and spinach.

Choosing the Right Food

Pigs eat anything that they find. It is true that pigs can eat fruits and vegetables but that doesn't mean you can feed your pig lots of fruits. Fruits should be given in a small quantity. Choose a high-quality formulated pig feed from the stores. You can take suggestions from your pet store and buy a pig food that is healthy and nutritious. Apart from formulated feed, you can also feed vegetables and fruits to pigs but in controlled quantity. You can give your pig tops and bottoms of beans, the rind from a soft melon, the core of a head of lettuce, etc. grains are the main source of carbohydrates for pigs, but grains alone cannot provide your pig with a complete nutrition.

Why You Should Not Try Feeding Dog/Cat Food?

Cat food is for cats and dog food is for a dog. That's why avoid feeding your pet pig food meant for other animals. Human food items cannot be fed to pigs because they have salt and preservatives in it which is harmful for pigs. Pigs are omnivore, which means that they will require a balanced diet of vegetables and protein. Too much protein intake can also damage the system of a pig and create weight problems. Moreover, avoid feeding your pet pigs food for swine breed. Swine feed is rich in proteins which will be harmful for your pet pig.

Automatic Feeders and Free Feeding

If you can't maintain a proper feeding schedule for your pet pig then buy an automatic or electric feeder. Automatic feeders are very efficient as they let you set the time, amount of food, and water that you want your pet pig to get. These automatic feeders control the timing and the amount of food fed. This makes it extremely easy for the owners to get hold of their pet pig's feeding schedule. This works extremely well when you are out of home and you want your pet pig to be fed on time.

Water is Essential

Pigs need to stay hydrated as they do not sweat. Especially in summers when the weather is hot, pigs will easily get dehydrated if not provided with excess clean water. As much as drinking water is vital for your pig to stay hydrated, you can also leave it in a water pool. Pig's skin gets sun burnt and the heat extracts all the water from their body. That's why your pig will also need to cool itself down by laying in a pool of water.

Where to get the Food Online?

Pigs are omnivores and can eat veggies and meat. Therefore, feeding a pet pig is not a huge concern for owners. Pig owners can find pig feed on the market and they can also feed them home-cooked meals. The easiest way to get pig food is through an online website. There are several online stores that sell pig food

- www.mazuri.com
- www.millbryhill.co.uk
- www.amazon.co.uk
- www.amazon.com
- www.tractorsupply.com
- www.nutrenaworld.com

3) Accommodating a Pet Pig

Accommodating a pet pig in your home is not as easy as many might anticipate. You have to design their living area in such a way that it includes both; indoors and outdoors. As much as your pig likes to sleep on a bed, wrapped up in a blanket, it also has physical needs such as exercise, walk, and running. These are certain considerations that you need to make before your pet pig arrives. As an owner, you have to meet your pet pig's requirements by providing it a perfect home to live in.

Sleep Area

Pigs are extremely territorial that's why it is better to give them a particular area of your home which they can rule. The area of your home that you give your pet must have its bedding, food, and litter. You can keep wooden beds for pigs with soft blankets on them. Pigs love to sleep under blankets and will feel more comfortable hiding inside it for long naps. You can also add pillows to your pigs. There are small tents available in stores that can serve as great beds for pigs.

"Business" Area

Pigs do not like to get messy when it comes to their property. They do not litter their sleeping area and will need a litter box away from their bed. You can put a litter box with non-toxic soil in the corner of their room. Once you define their poo area, they will start going there for their business.

Exercise Area

Pigs need lots of exercise and physical activity to stay healthy and fit. An exercise area is usually designed in the outdoor area of the home where your pig can run around, jump and play. Set an exercise routine for your pig, take it for a morning walk, play with it, etc and keep it healthy. Exercise can also include games. You can hide your pig's favorite toy in your yard and let it find it. An important thing to consider when designing the exercise area outdoors is to create an enclosure or install strong fences. Pigs are curious by nature and love to escape. They are strong and they might try to break the fence and run outside. Train your pig to walk on a leash to avoid odd behaviors.

Socialization Arena

In the initial days of your pig at its new home, it will feel shy and uncomfortable. Your pig might be afraid of the surroundings and other family members. That's why it is extremely essential for you to bond with your pig the right way. Too much socialization will scare your new pet pig and too little might put him under depression.

Pigs crave company, which means you will need to give them proper time so that they do not get bored and destructive. Let your pig roam freely around the areas of the home that are not harmful for it. Give your pig time to get familiar with the environment and the other members of your family. To make your pig comfortable in less time, guide your family members to maintain a distance from the pig so that it doesn't get scared. Avoid touching your pig too much as it will irritate it.

Define areas of socialization for your pet pig as there will be areas that will not be suitable for it. The socialization area should be free of any harmful substances, tools, surfaces, and products. If you have slippery marble flooring then put a carpet over it to keep your pig from slipping and falling.

If you have other pets in your home, make sure you make them familiar with your pet pig in its initial days. This will make the pig realize that those animals are harmless and can be trusted. Your pig will make friends with cats and dogs. Avoid leaving your pet pig and dog together because they can get into fights.

4) Traveling Concerns

Pigs are harmless animals but different countries have different travelling laws for them. We have heard people travelling from one place to another with their cats and dogs but not many people know about traveling concerns for pet pigs.

- To be able to travel safely with your pig, you will need to make it used to a kennel or crate.
- If travelling outside town, contact USDA to get a travelling pass for your pet pig.
- You might need to submit a medical certificate and blood test reports to the department and carry it with you to avoid any problems.

Keeping an Eye on Local Regulations

- Before taking your pig outside or for travelling purposes, check with your community's zoning laws because exotic pets like pigs are not allowed in the open.
- Some local regulations do not allow pigs to be near neighbor's homes.
- Pigs should be kept 2 meter away from a home's boundary wall or fence.
- Pig owners should keep an eye on their pet and prevent it from escaping.
- Owners should prevent their pigs from damaging the environment and hurting humans.
- Pigs are not allowed to roam around freely or disturb other people in a community.

Travelling Safe

- Whenever taking your pet pig outside the house, make sure you have undertaken proper safety measures to not only ensure the pig's safety but other's too.
- While travelling with your pig in your car, do not let it sit on your back seat.
- Keep your pig in a crate while transporting it.
- If you are travelling to another country, make sure that you book an airline that allows pets and keeps them safe.
- Do not take a risk with your pets while travelling, as many countries don't allow pigs to be imported from other countries because they are categorized as swine animals.
- If you will travel to a place where there are laws against pigs, your pig will be taken away.
- Get a dog ramp for your pig, which allows your pig to climb on your SUV's back without getting hurt.
- Adjust the length of the ramp.

5) Daily Grooming Guidelines

Pigs aren't furry, so they usually stay clean but that doesn't mean that you should stop grooming them. Pigs have light hair on their body and their skin is soft and sensitive. They will often require some cleaning and caring for their fragile skin. The basic grooming for your pet pig will include cleaning and maintaining the ears, hooves, tusk, skin, and eyes. Read on to some tips on your pet pig's grooming.

- Clean your pet pig's eyes on a daily basis because water from the eyes can make them look dirty. Use a soft damp cloth to clear the dirt off.
- Ears also need a lot of maintenance as wax builds up quickly. Use Q-tips to gently clean your pig's ears.
- Use a non-slip bath pad while bathing or grooming your pig so it doesn't slip or fall.
- Give your pet pig a tick check daily.

- Use a tick powder.
- Brush your pig on a daily basis. It will not only love the scratching but will also stay clean.
- Apply skin lotion daily because a pig's skin is sensitive to sun and can easily get irritated.
- You will not need to bathe your pig on a regular basis as pigs are clean animals and excessive bathing can harm their skin.

Chapter 11: Training Your Pet Pig

Your new pet pig will get used to the rules of your house with help of lots of training. Pigs are intelligent animals that learn things quickly. They also understand different voice expressions of their owners. That's why it will not take them a lot of time to get used to your house rules. Moreover, you will need to shower your pig with treats so that it feels appreciated for the right behavior.

1) Your Pet Needs Training

Every pet needs training so that it becomes easier for it and the people around it to adjust. However, pigs are little different from other pets. They are extremely clever. So don't think that your training will go to waste. It is a fact that pigs are extremely loving but it is also true that they can become extremely moody and aggressive at times. That's why owners need to realize that training a pet pig is extremely essential for everyone's safety.

2) Training Basics

The most basic training your pet pig will need when it comes to your home is litter training. A pig usually doesn't go around peeing and pooping the house but it will need the initial training to get used to a litter box. Pigs pee and poo in a corner far from their sleeping area, so make sure you have kept a litter box in your pig's room. Apart from the basic litter training, you will need to train your pig to behave. Sometimes pigs get angry when they are bored or hungry and start damaging the property. To avoid such incidents, it is better to train your pig in the beginning. Keep in mind the positive trait of a pig i.e. it is a very intelligent animal. With help of training, your pig will start to follow the rules set by you as the owner and the boss of the house.

You will also need to make your pig understand the word 'NO'. Pigs love food and will chew upon anything they find. That's why you will often catch your pig eating things off the ground. To make this habit stop, you will need to say No to your pig. When you will say it in an angry tone and after a few warnings, it will understand. You can also tap its head with a light hand to tell it that it is not appreciated.

When pigs are unhappy or bored, they will become destructive. This is another thing that you will need to stop. For this, you have to make sure that your pig knows what's right and what's not. Over a course of a few days, it will start to learn. To appreciate you pig when it learns something, give it a treat. Your pig will understand that it is a sign of appreciation and will start to follow the rules.

3) Acclimatization to the Leash

Leash and harness training is extremely essential for a pig but it is also crucial, as many pigs don't react well to it. A leash is meant for the protection of your pig and others in an open environment. Do not force your pig to wear a leash as it will become aggressive. Pigs are prey and that's why their nature is to protect themselves when they feel threatened. When you make your pig wear a leash and take it out for a walk, it will feel frightened and would want to hide or run. However, having a harness or leash on, it will feel as if it is being forced. That's why you will need to train your pig first.

Leash training will start off with you trying to make your pig familiar with it. Go near your pig with a leash and touch it. Once your pig feels comfortable, you can bring the leash closer to it. If it doesn't react, there shall be no problem. However, if it reacts badly, make sure you take the harness away from it immediately. While trying to make your pig wear the harness, you should bring treats with you for distraction. If your pig starts to get rid of the harness, offer it a treat so that it calms down and understands that you are not going to harm it. There will be a lot of touching and scratching while you try to put the harness on because physical contact calms pigs.

If you were successful in making your pig wear a leash, it is time to teach it how it works. Once the pig wears the leash, it will feel scared and will show aggressive behavior. Hold the leash and pull it a little. If your pig feels uncomfortable, offer a treat and put it on the ground. A leash can scare a pig, so it will need to feel safe and for that you will need to prove to your pig that it is safe with you. Leave the leash and let your pig roam around freely and put some food on the ground so that it comes running towards you. Again hold its leash, pull it and let it go. Repeating this technique will make the pig feel safe and it will know that it is not restricted and can move around at its own will.

4) *Walking*

Pigs are playful animals that love to walk and play around. That's why it is really important to take them for a walk and improve their physical health. However, you cannot just go out on the road with your pet pig. As pig owners, you will need to get a pig walking license from your local animal office. Many countries do not allow pigs to be seen out without a license that's why get registered and mention your walking route. Once your request has been approved, you will be provided with the license and you can take your pig for a walk.

With the help of the leash and harness training, you will also be able to train your pig to walk. Walking is essential for a pig's physical health and bones. You can take your pig for a walk in the park or your neighborhood if you train it to stay calm. Again, walking means your pig will be controlled by you and will make it aggressive. However, if you have already trained your pig for the leash, it will be easier for you to take it for a walk.

The hardest part is to train your pig to walk at your pace. For this purpose, you will need to have lots of treat with you. Walk in a normal pace and if your pig runs ahead of you, call it with a polite tone and show it a treat. When it comes close to you, start walking again. When your pig starts to follow you and comes close to you, offer it some treats. Train your pig in the similar way continuously and even for days. Eventually, in a few days time, your pig will learn to walk at your pace. Remember not to force your pig into learning something that it is uncomfortable with. You can only train your pig to learn something if you adopt a polite tone and offer lots of treats.

5) Penalizing Unwanted Behavior

Pigs do get aggressive when they are bored, deprived of food or love. That's why as an owner, you will need to avoid things that would give a rise to its unwanted and aggressive behavior. When pigs get aggressive, they usually bite, push, destruct property, and threatening other individuals. This can become uncontrollable if proper training hasn't been conducted. However, creating a more reinforced controlling strategy, you will only make your pig's behavior worst.

Firstly, you need to find out the right reason for your pig's unusual or aggressive behavior. Your pig can get aggressive if it doesn't get what it wants; food, toy, treat, etc. Do not try to control your pig's behavior by dominating. If the pig is getting out of control and becoming a threat to its surroundings, make sure you try to divert its attention to yourself. It is best to adopt a positive reinforcement strategy that involves a lot of treats, rubbing and scratching. When your pig is acting out, give it a back scratch and do things that it finds positive. This will give out a message to your pig that you are not harmful. However, to ensure that the pig doesn't pick this behavior as a habit, you will need to tell your pig that it is wrong by saying words that it can relate to.

Another tactic to control a pig's aggressive behavior is by outing it in its comfort zone; its room or playing area. You can also try to ignore its behavior by simply walking away from the situation. This will make the pig feel that its behavior is unwanted. If you are having troubles with your pig's behavior, remember that pigs are extremely intelligent and will follow the rules and directions given to them by their owners.

6) Maintaining Your Patience

During the entire training process of your pet pig, you will need to be very patient. Pigs are clever but they will need time to adjust to your rules. It is important that owners adopt a positive reinforcement strategy to train their pet pigs or else they'll end up making it aggressive. Alongside patience, you will need help of some other things to ensure that the pig learns in a positive environment. You will need lots of treats, toys, cuddling, and hugging to train it properly. The owners that lack patience often get furious on their pigs. They yell and hit the pig without realizing the consequences. A pig that is treated with aggression, adopts an aggressive behavior.

Pigs are extremely sensitive and react badly to aggression. Even when you are upset or infuriated at your pig, do not at any point yell or hit it. Pigs that get treated this way often become violent. That's why it is extremely important for pig owners to realize that pigs can only be treated with patience.

7) Consistency and Perseverance

Training your pig with consistency and perseverance is also very important. Your pig will learn new tricks and rules only when you keep trying. If you give up in the middle of the training process, your pig will never listen to you. Consistent training is also very important for making the pig learn the right thing. If you adopt one strategy at one time and another strategy at some other time, your pig will get confused. It will take a little time training your new pet pig, but patience and consistency will get you to it faster.

8) Using Hand Signals and Speech

The training process of a pig involves a lot of hand and speech signals. There will be times when it will become harder for you handle your pig's aggression. The pigs that are assertive will need hand and voice signals to stop acting up.

- If your pig is aiming to hit someone, a child or a friend, grab it from the back and push it away.
- Push your pig around the shoulders to distract it from its target.
- Do not squeeze your pig's neck trying to push it away as it will make the situation worse.
- Clap with your hands to interrupt the pig from doing something unusual.
- Loud sounds like the one of a clap really help diverting a pig's mind from its intent.
- Loud sounds also give out the message that you are the boss and this attitude is intolerable.
- Take help from a sorting board i.e. a wooden or plastic shield with holes in it meant for protection from physical threat.
- If you see that you pig is aggressive and can charge at you any moment, use a sorting board as a shield and push it backwards to tell your pig that you are serious.
- You can stamp your feet loudly to scare the pig and to tell it that enough is enough.
- Adopt a confidence tone while scolding your pig.
- It is best to keep your pet pig in its room when visitors are in the house.
- If your pig doesn't take speech signals too well, try adopting a different strategy.
- Physical correction is one the best way to stop your pig from behaving badly.
- Do not train your pet pig to take food from your hand as it will bite your hand.

9) Teaching Tricks

Teaching your pigs different tricks is part of the training program. You will need to be patient and consistent while training different tricks to your pig. However, you cannot be forceful towards your pig as it will get aggressive.

- You should start by calling your pig's name.

- If it doesn't listen or is distracted, throw a treat at it.
- Always train your pet in private and in a less distracted environment.
- For the training process to go smoothly you will need to be bonded to your pig or else it will not feel comfortable.
- Teach one trick at a time.
- Start teaching simple tricks to your pig first.
- Teach it to sit, shake hands, and fetch.
- Whenever your pig learns a trick and obeys your command, offer a treat.
- Do not prolong the training session as pigs get bored very easily.
- To make your pig learn to sit, you will need to hold a treat in your hands and kneel in front of it. Now hold the treat just above your pig's snout and say 'sit'. Then bring the treat back and gently push the pig's back making it sit. When the pig sits, give it a treat and praise.
- To make your pig learn to shake hands, you will need to kneel in front of your pig with a treat in your hands. Pick its right hand and say 'shake hands'. Give your pig the treat and appreciate it so that it follows. Repeat this a several times until it learns to shake hands.

10) House Training or House "Breaking"

Housebreaking a pig simply means toilet training. If you do not train your pig to defecate in a particular spot or area, you are going to find pig poops all over the house, except for the pig's sleeping area. Pigs are not messy and will never defecate near their sleeping area. However, if the pig wasn't trained when it was young, it will become messy and poop wherever it feels like. This is a huge problem that pig owners should address in the initial days of the pig at home.

- When your pig has had its meal, make sure that you take it to its poo spot or to your backyard.

- You can make the pig wear a harness so that it stays in your control.
- Wait for a few minutes until your pig finally defecates.
- As soon as the pig defecates, offer a little treat to it.
- The treat will mark a reward for defecating in the outdoors.
- You pig will not learn this trick until repeated several times.
- Once your pig connects treats with defecating in the backyard or its designated spot, it will always defecate outside.
- For night time, keep a litter box inside the pig's room.
- Teach the pig to poo in the litter box using the same technique.
- Remember, repetition is the key here and it will make it easier for your pig to learn the trick.
- If your pig is unable to learn, do not force it.
- Apply another positive reinforcement strategy instead of being harsh to your pig.
- If you have a fear that your pig will mess your home at night time, confine it to a room instead of letting it roam around the entire house.

11) Simple Tips and Tricks for Training

To make your pet pig learn new tricks and follow your rules, you will need to come up with a different approach.

- Always have cheerios or grapes as treats for your pig.
- Be polite.
- Do not over feed your pig with treats as it will not get trained.
- Replace treats with toys in the later stage of training.
- Make your pig comfortable before starting its training.
- Use short words while training.
- Do not change the words as it will confuse your pig.
- When using voice commands, make sure your tone is polite yet authoritative.
- If your pig bites at you to get treats, do not offer treats.

- Train your pig to pick treats from the ground instead of offering with your hands.
- Keep an eye on your pig during the night as it is likely to poo at night.
- Know when to say NO.
- Appreciate your pig if it obeys you.
- Don't bore the pig by dragging the training session.
- Keep your pig happy.
- Do not adopt a harsh tone with your pig.
- Be consistent in teaching tricks to your pig.
- Train your pig in an area it's comfortable in.
- Most importantly, be patient.

12) Handling Accidents While Training

Some pigs are more assertive than others and show temper tantrums when being trained or simply ignored. Pigs can become really aggressive only when they feel lonely or are deprived of food. They need their owner's attention and when they don't get it, they start destroying things in their surroundings. Proper safety measures and precautions should be taken when training your pig. If your pig gets aggressive and comes charging at you or bites you, take protection from the sorting board or wear gloves.

Accidents also occur when you have other pets in your home. Pigs usually get along with everyone and are very social. However, one shouldn't forget that pigs are prey and that's why they get threatened. When pigs feel threatened, they react with aggression. This behavior often causes problems when you leave your pig with your dogs. Usually, a pig will be the one to start the fight as it will grunt at the dog. To avoid such situations, make sure you keep all the pets together under your supervision.

Chapter 12: Medical Concerns

Pigs, like other pet animals, have different health and medical concerns. This entirely depends on the environment the pig lives in. It is an owner's responsibility to take care of their pets. If you provide quality food, water, enclosure, hygiene, and medical care, the pig will never get sick.

1) Why Is A Pig More Prone to Illness?

Pigs need proper care and attention to stay healthy. This means that it is important for the owners of the pigs to provide them with proper food, preventative care, routine checkups and vaccinations. Pigs are prone to illness because they are easily affected by the weather. In winters, pigs get pneumonia, and in summers they get dehydrated.

Pigs love to bathe in a pool of mud which carries a lot of bacteria and germs which can easily infect them, as pigs have sensitive skin. Pigs get most affected by influenza which is contagious and can harm human health. However, the risks of flu commonly occur in swine breeds that live in very poor conditions.

2) Common Health Risks

There are some common health problems in pigs that can be controlled with a preventative approach. A pig that lives in a healthy and sound environment is less likely to get sick.

Digestive disorders

Young pigs have diarrhea problems due to the change in diet. Pigs take time to adjust to new food and when your pig is under the effect of diarrhea, make sure it has a lot of clean water to drink. Diarrhea can also cause dehydration which leads to severe health risks for pigs. Call a vet in case the diarrhea gets worst. Another reason for digestive problems in pigs is that they have a huge appetite.

Arthritis

Just like humans, old pigs might develop arthritis and begin to have joint problems. Pigs eat a lot and get fat. So, when these pigs get old, their joints are not able to handle the weight of their body, as a result weakening the joints and in worst cases fractures. Arthritis is very painful and preventative care should be taken to protect the pig.

Parasites

Parasites like fleas, ticks and mange can crawl up your pig's body and cause various infections and health problems. Consult a vet and buy parasite powders to get rid of them.

Exotic diseases

Pigs are classified as swine animals but the pigs that you bring home belong to other breeds including pot bellied, tea-cup pigs and other mini pigs. Swine breeds have a threat of catching exotic diseases like mouth and foot disease and swine flu which are extremely harmful to human health and are contagious in nature.

Pneumonia

Pneumonia in pigs is caused by viruses and bacteria. A pig that is infected with pneumonia needs immediate attention and medical care. If you see signs of pneumonia in your pig, contact your vet to get pneumonia shots.

Obesity

Pigs are excessive eaters and would eat anything from vegetables to fruits ad meat. That's why many of them suffer from obesity. Obesity is harmful for a pig's overall health and puts its heart in danger. Don't over feed your pig and make sure your pig gets enough physical exercise required to stay fit.

Respiratory illness

Nasal infections are common in pigs especially the little ones. A runny nose means your pig has nasal infection. In most cases, nasal infections are not very concerning but in many cases the infection worsens and causes permanent nose deformities. With help of regular vaccinations, pigs can be protected from respiratory illnesses.

Constipation

Constipation is not very common in pigs. However, keep an eye on your pig's excretion and if you find signs of blood strains, know that it has constipation. Constipation occurs due to lack of water in the body and when the pig eats foreign objects. Make sure that the pig has clean water to drink and do not let your pig eat random things off the floor. Constipation can be cured with help of medication. However, prolonged straining might damage the rectal area of the pig which will need to be removed surgically.

Urinary tract issues

Pigs often get bladder stones and infections. Always watch your pig's activities as it might have a health concern. If your pig is in pain while it urinates, take it to a vet. Bladder infection can easily be cured with the help of medications and antibiotics. If the infection prolongs for a longer period of time, visit your vet. Bladder stones often cause urinary problems which need to be removed surgically.

Skin problems

Melanoma and sunburns are common skin problems in pigs. Pigs have sensitive skin that gets affected by the heat of the sun. Sunburn makes the skin itchy and dry. Use a moisturizing lotion on your pig's skin to prevent the skin condition from getting worse. However, melanomas can get pretty big and spread quickly. So, keep an eye on abnormal growths and consult your vet and get them removed.

Fractures

Pigs are prone to getting fractures, as they are naturally curious. If you have furniture in your home that your pet pig can easily jump on, immediately remove it. Moreover, install carpet and non-slip floors in your home so that your pig doesn't fall. When pigs fall or jump from height, their bones get injured. These injured bones are very painful. Consult your vet in case of bone fractures and remove all hazardous objects from your home.

Brain Injuries and Nerve Disorders

Brain diseases, spinal injuries and nerve disorders are caused by lack of water and environmental factors. If your pig is confined in a small cage with dirt all around, there is a high chance that its brain will get damaged. If you live near a factory, the fumes and chemicals can harm your pig. Overheating is another cause of brain and nerve injury. Make sure you provide a small pool to your pig, a bowl with clean water and bathe it in summers to keep it cool.

3) Pig Vaccinations

Vaccinations are essential for a pig's health and are highly effective in boosting the immune system. Immune system is responsible for fighting different diseases and their infections inside the body. When any living being gets under the influence of a disease or virus, its immune system begins to weaken. With a weak immune system, it becomes harder for the body to fight against harmful viruses, causing serious medical conditions and in worst cases; death.

Vaccines contain antigens that are from the virus. These bacteria go inside the body and stimulate an immune response that helps in curing the condition. The vaccines are given to the pigs through injection.

There are different types of vaccines; one that multiplies the number of viruses inside the body and another that brings down the number of bacteria. In some cases, the decreased number of bacteria cures the disease and in other, maximizing the number helps prolong the immunity. However, if these vaccines get exposed to heat or harmful bacteria, they will not cure the disease.

Vaccines that are meant for respiratory or intestinal diseases are not as effective as the vaccines given for generalized or systematic diseases. A vaccine that doesn't work might have been infected, damaged, exposed, etc. That's why it is extremely important that owners consult a highly professional vet for vaccinations.

4) The Initial Exam

Buying a pet pig is a lot of responsibility. Pigs need proper care and health check-ups to stay healthy. Your job starts before your bring your pet pig home. When you buy a pig from a pet shop, first thing you need to do is get it checked by an experienced vet. An initial check-up is a must for pigs as they can easily get sick. A visit to the vet will provide you complete information through a physical examination of the pig you are about to bring home. The vet will examine its oral and physical health to ensure that the pig doesn't have any flu, virus, health conditions, etc. Once you get a green signal from your vet that the pig is perfectly healthy, you can then bring it home. The vet will vaccinate your pig with the necessary vaccinations. In the initial exam of your pig, the vet will check it for worms, skin infections, hooves trimming, and much more.

5) Regular Check-Ups Are Important!

Preventative care is very essential for your pet pig. To ensure that your pig stays perfectly healthy, you will need to visit a professional vet frequently. The disadvantage of not seeing a vet is that many times a minor problem becomes huge. Causing harm to the pig and resulting in a lot of money. Preventative maintenance also includes grooming your pet pig.

6) The Vaccination Schedule

To get your pig's check-up done, you need to visit an experienced vet. Ask friends and family and visit a vet that is trusted. Sometimes vets over-vaccinate a pig that is harmful for their health. The typical vaccination for a pig given on a yearly basis include; Bordatella, Erysipelas, and Pasturella. These vaccines are injected with a double dose the first time. A pig's vaccines are different than other pet animals like cats and dogs. So beware of any vet that is giving a doubtful vaccine to your pig. A pig's vaccination schedule depends upon the state laws you are residing in. every state has different vaccination requirements for pigs.

Vaccinations for Piglets

Vaccination dosage, schedule and type are different for piglets as they are sensitive and under a threat of catching different diseases. Just a week after birth, a piglet gets its first vaccine. The vaccines given to a pet pig are; Pneumonia, Rhinitis, Erysipelas, and Mycoplasma. If you miss any of these vaccines you pig might suffer from bone disfigurement or other skin infections which can be lethal.

- At 3 weeks of age, piglets should be vaccinated for swine virus. The vaccines given to piglets are to strengthen their immune system to fight different diseases and viruses. At 4 weeks, piglets should be vaccinated with boosters of Rhinitis, Pneumonia, Erysipelas, and Mycoplasma.
- At 8 weeks, piglets should be vaccinated with a parasite that fights Glasser's disease, Actinobacillus, Deworm, Mycoplasma, Erysipeias, Bordetella, and Pasturella.
- At 9 to 11 weeks, your pig will need to be vaccinated for TGE, 6-way Lepto, Mycoplasma, Erysipeias, Bordetella, Pasturella, Deworm, and Actinobacillus.

Vaccines for Adult Pigs

The vaccination schedule for adult pigs is different than that of piglets. Adult pigs need to be protected from different viruses and diseases. Although their vaccination schedule is less aggressive than young pigs because they have a stronger immune system.

- The vaccines should be repeated every six months for pigs that are kept in a herd.
- The pigs that live alone should be given these vaccines on a yearly basis.
- Rabies is a virus that is not harmful to a pig and a pig's immune system is capable of fighting it. So, it is less likely that your pig will need a rabies shot.
- Oral vaccines in the form of a pill can be given to pigs by hiding it inside their food.

The schedule for your pig's vaccine depends upon a number of factors. First of all, your state's requirements for pathogens and whether your pig lives with a herd of pigs or not. Pigs that live in a herd are prone to catching diseases and viruses. A vaccine is injected in a pig's butt muscle or 2 – 3 inches behind the ears. You might see certain side-effects of the vaccine that fade away within 24 hours. The pig might feel dizzy after getting injected.

7) Tips for Choosing a Veterinarian

Vet-hunt should start days before you bring your new pet pig home. A vet is the most important person you will start to see a lot once you get a pig. Pigs need a lot of care and maintenance and for this very reason you will need to get in touch with an experienced veterinarian. Do not choose a vet that you don't know about. It is always best to ask people who have had experience with pigs. Visit the vets that others recommend you.

Another important thing to consider when you are vet-hunting is the degree and certificate of your vet with the veterinary association of your state. The vet should be registered with your state which will be a proof of his/her authenticity.

Below is a list of questions that you must ask yourself before confirming a vet for your pet pig.

- Is the vet new to the business?
- Has he/she been associated with a friend or a family member in the past?
- Does the vet treat every breed differently or does the vet consider all pigs as the same?
- Does the vet allow owners to be around their pig while in the surgery or getting shots?
- Does your vet allow you to ask questions from him/her?
- Is the vet open to suggestions and questions? (If your vet doesn't answer your questions, it is time to switch.)
- Does the vet treats and handles the animals in a good way or does he apply force while vaccinating? (If the vet gets aggressive or applies force on your struggling pig, do not continue with that vet.)
- Does the vet have a strong history of pets and a sound background?

If all of the above questions are answered correctly, you will be able to decide on a vet. Make sure you do not choose a vet that harms your pig or doesn't have a soft corner for pet animals. A vet that is perfect for your pet pig will be the one that is willing to answer all your questions and making you feel comfortable. do not hesitate in asking yourself these questions as it is the matter of your pig's safety and health.

When you take your pet pig to a vet for the first time, make sure you keep your eyes and mind open. The first visit to the vet will reveal a lot of things about the clinic and the vet's experience. Sit for a while and observe the environment and the staff at the clinic. Check the clinic for hygiene and cleanliness because a dirty clinic means harm to your pet pig. Check the equipment at the clinic. Evaluate the entire place to see if the place is clean, odor free and well-managed.

The thing that helps the most in choosing the right vet is recommendations from friends and family. Before making an appointment at the vet, you should opt for family, friends and neighbors that have had pets or pigs before. These people are experienced and will give you a better idea and advice on picking a vet for your pet pig. Based upon the opinion of these people, you can then easily choose a good vet for your pet pig.

Beware!! Many vets and clinics invest a lot of money in advertising, TV commercials, banners, press ads, etc. Heavy advertising doesn't prove that the vet is authentic. Many times clinics attract pet owners through advertising tactics. Some of these clinics and vets are ill experienced. That's why it is always best to take recommendations from people who have experience with pet pigs.

8) Maintain Medical Reports

Maintaining medical records of your pet pigs is extremely essential for a pig's safety and health. These medical reports help in a number of ways especially when your pet pig needs treatment. These records help in determining the type of treatment your pet pig requires. Pig owners should have a copy of their pig's medical reports to help them in case of emergencies. A medical file of your pet pig should be carried while travelling.

Keep a complete medical history of your pet pig that includes its visit to the vets, vaccinations, medical condition, previous surgeries, etc since the time of its birth. If you have bought it from someone else, make sure you ask for its medical file. If the previous owner doesn't have the pig's medical records, get its check-up done when you bring it home.

If you are adopting or buying a pet from a shelter or a pet shop, don't forget to ask for a copy of its medical records. These medical records will help you keep a track of your pig's vaccines, medical conditions, and much more. To ensure that your pet pig stays healthy, a medical history is a must to have.

Medical reports are also helpful when you are travelling out of the city. Many states have different rules against pet animals, especially pigs as they are categorizes as swine animals. However, if you have a fully maintained medical history of your pet pig, you will be able to clear the confusions and prove to the authorities that your pig is perfectly healthy.

If you are moving to a new place, you will need to change your vet. This means that a new vet that is completely unknown to your pet pig will handle it. In such situations, owners should ask for the medical file of their pig from its previous vet. You may also take the contact information of your old vet and provide it to your new vet so that in case of any consultation or queries, the vet can ask the old vet. The medical history that you give your new vet will help him/her deal with your pet pig in a better way. Your pet pig's medical care is as important as your own, so be vigilant and adopt a pro-active approach.

The medical records of your pet pig should contain:

- A record of each visit to the vet.
- A complete history of any treatment, vaccination, medication and dose.
- A complete record of the tests conducted on the pig including blood cultures, ultrasounds, x-rays, etc.
- Complete information on any surgeries done on the pig.
- Record of all hospital stays.
- Record of progress and side-effects of any medication or surgery done on the pig.

9) Neutering and Spaying

Neutering and spaying holds a lot of importance when you have a pet pig roaming around in your house. An un-neutered male or female pig can become a real problem for owners. An un-neutered male will become sexually mature and active at the age of 2 months. These male pigs will then start to hump everything in sight which will be really unpleasant to watch. Moreover, sexually active pigs have a certain odor that does not feel right. When male pigs are excited, they will get more aggressive towards everyone in the surrounding, especially if you have any female pigs.

Females also act like male pigs when they are sexually active. When a female pig turns 5 months old, she begins her heat cycle which is a menstruation cycle. Whenever your female pig will come on heat, she will start to pee in open spaces to spread her scent which will attract make pigs. A typical heat cycle comes once every month and lasts 2-3 days. In this period, your female pig will run around the house aggressively and would try to escape. So, owners with sexually active pigs are advised to build strong fences around their home's boundary.

Male pigs can be neutered when they turn 1 month old. However, it is best to get the procedure done when they gain a little mass on their body. The male piglet should weigh around 10 – 12lbs at the time of neutering. A male pig's testicles, especially a potbellied is not visible. Consult an expert vet who has experience of neutering males because sometimes both the testicles are not removed completely, resulting in a failed neuter attempt. Many pigs also become herniated after the procedure, so make sure you get in touch with the best vet in town.

A female's neutering procedure is much more complicated than a male pig's. The ideal time for neutering a female pig is after one menstrual cycle. Female pigs cannot be neutered after the age of 8 months. An 8 month old female pig weighs a lot and due to their thick fat, the surgery becomes very risky. An un-neutered female pig will have the urge to reproduce and not given the chance, it will become really aggressive and destructive. The effect of hormones during a female pig's heat cycle reflects in her mood and behavior.

If you are planning to buy a pet pig, make sure that it is neutered. If not, consult a vet immediately and get it neutered before you bring it home. Un-neutered pigs become a trouble for owners. The best companions are the pigs that are neutered or spayed as they have less mood swings.

The Process of Neutering

Many vets lack the experience of neutering or spaying pet pigs. A vet that is not familiar with neutering might give you wrong advice and conduct risky surgeries. It is important for owners to do their research and know all about neutering of pet pigs. This will help them keep their pet pigs safe from any injuries and health risks. Below is some information that will prove to be helpful while talking to a vet for neutering your pig.

- During the process of neutering, a vet should use ISO Fluorine Gas.
- Younger pigs of 150lbs or less are masked with oxygen or ISO Fluorine Gas according to their size.
- Older pigs that are heavier and hard to handle are injected with Rompan and Tealazol mixture.
- The correct dosage of Rompan is; 1mg/pound.
- The correct dosage for Tealazol is; 2mg/pound.
- Rompan and Tealazol mixture is injected using a syringe in the neck or in the butt muscle.
- Blunt dissection is preferred for the procedure.
- Cutting the tissue can lead to excessive blood loss.
- The exterior inguinal ring in males should be closed with sutures of 2-0 vicryl to prevent hernia after the anesthetic affect fades away.
- The exterior inguinal ring should be closed after the removal of each testicle.
- After the procedure is completed, the pig should be injected with Procaine Penicillin which is an anti-biotic that fights several bacterial infections.

Talk to your vet in detail before getting your pig neutered and make sure that the vet follows the right procedure using the right dosage and medicine.

Advantages of Neutering and Spaying

Neutering your pet pig is the best option to have an extremely loving companion. Un-neutered pigs are aggressive, destructive, harmful, and feel depressed most of the time. To establish a real bond with your pet pig, you will need to go with the option of neutering or spaying. Read on to the list below that will provide you solid reasons to choose neutering.

- Neutered male and female pigs are less likely to get aggressive, destructive and are less harmful to others, including the owner itself.
- Neutered male pigs don't have a risk of developing prostate cancer.
- Neutered males will not smell bad.
- Neutered males will not develop testicular cancers.
- Neutered male and female pigs will not get into meaningless fights.
- Neutered pigs have a higher chance of getting a new home.
- It is easy to control neutered pigs as they will not multiply in number.
- Spayed females are less likely to develop mammary cancers.
- Spayed females will not develop urinary infections.
- Female pigs that are spayed are less likely to develop ovarian cancer.
- Spayed female pigs will not urinate everywhere in the house.
- Spayed female pig is more affectionate and is less likely to have abrupt mood swings.
- Spayed and neutered male and female pigs will not try to escape all the time.
- Spayed and neutered pigs are happier pets.
- Neutered pigs will not mark territories.
- Neutered pigs are easier to control and train.

- Neutered pig's personality is calmer than that of an un-neutered pig. That's why they become better companions to their owners.

10) De-Worming

Before we get into the whole de-worming or worming procedure for pigs, we need to know what causes intestinal mites, mange and much more.

What are Mange Mites?

Mange affects more than 60% of the pigs in different countries around the world. Mange is the name of a parasite that irritates and damages the skin of a pig. This skin disease is caused by two mites named Sarcoptes scabiei and Demodex phylloides. Sarcoptic mites cause a lot of damage to a pig's skin. The irritation caused by them makes the pig scratch its skin. When a pig scratches its skin, it becomes damaged and wounded. Mange also creates diet problems and makes the pig depressed.

Mange is contagious as it spreads from one pig to another. The cause of spread may be contact of contaminated substance or direct skin contact with the infected pig. A pig that has mange mites will have red spots in its skin.

Getting Rid of Mange

Mange can be put to a stop by a number of ways; spraying your pet pig, applying a lotion containing 20% phosmet to the skin of its back, injecting medicine with syringe, or adding the medicine in the feed.

Some of the prescribed dosage to eradicate mange in pigs is:

- There are two types of medicines given to pigs with mange; Ivomec 1% solution and Dectomax.

- Ivomec is a parasiticide that controls and treats intestinal worms, lungworms, grubs, leech, and mange in pigs and other animals classified as cattle.
- The prescribed dosage is 200 mcg of ivermectin/kg of body weight of the pig.

Body Weight (lbs)	Volume (mL)
19	¼
38	½
75	1
150	2
225	3
300	4
375	5

- The injection of Ivomec should be given with a 16- or 18-gauge needle to protect the pig from infections.
- The injection should be given in the neck or in the skin behind the ears.
- Ivomec treatment should be given twice a year.
- Young pigs can be treated by spraying them with the medicine or applying the powder on their skin.

It is better to give your big the medicine orally instead of injecting because pigs get aggressive.

11) Poison Control

Owners are suggested to inspect their homes and remove any toxic chemicals or substances away from the reach of their pet pigs. Pigs love to chew on anything they find on the ground or near to them. That's why it is important to poison free your home.

However, trying so hard in cleaning your home of poisonous substances, your pig ends up eating the wrong things. That's when most of the owners freak out and do the wrong things which put their pig's life in danger.

There are certain foods and substances that can potentially harm a pig. It is extremely important that pig owners keep an emergency first-aid kit at their homes.

The Emergency First Aid Kit

There will be times when your pet pig will get injured or exposed to poisonous substances. The most important thing in such times is the emergency first-aid kit. The following things are a must in an emergency first-aid kit.

- A bulb syringe.
- Saline eye solution.
- Bottle of hydrogen peroxide, 3% USP.
- A turkey baster.
- A muzzle.
- A pet carrier.
- A can of pig food.
- Artificial tear gel.
- Forceps.
- Small thermometer.
- Stethoscope.
- Mild grease cutting dishwashing liquid.

If you have a kit packed with the above things, make sure you consult your vet and learn the directions of use.

The Immediate Response

When your pig ingests a poisonous substance, the first thing that most owners do is react badly. It is not the right time to panic as your pig is in a risky condition. You will need to calm down and take deep breaths for a few seconds and then think clearly.

The second step is to look for a first-aid kit (if you have one.)

Then you will need to call your vet or any emergency number like an ASPCA (Animal Poison Control Association)

If the vet isn't picking up, reach your nearest vet or rescue center.

Take the toxic substance with you so that the toxicologist can determine the damage caused by the substance.

Do not take too long fixing things on your own. Pig owners should have a rescue center's number and their vet's number with them. So, in case of an emergency, proper care and action can be taken.

What You Will Need

As owners of pet pigs, you must have the basic information of your animal.

- Its breed.
- Its age, sex, and weight.
- Its living conditions.
- Does it live alone or with other pigs?
- The symptoms noted after ingesting poisonous substance.
- The time of exposure.
- The product or substance that was ingested.

Preventative Measures

When you know what could harm your pig, you are actually preventing it from different incidents and health risks. Knowing all about a pig before you get one is the number one thing every owner should do. Conduct thorough research on your part and get to know all about your pet pig. A preventive approach will help you save your pig's life, medical bills and a lot of time.

The first thing to learn is the foods that are bad for a pet pig. As pig lovers and owners, we know that pigs love to eat and they are the ultimate foodies. They chew on anything they find on the ground and look up in bins to find food. That's why pig owners are advised to clean their homes before bringing a pig. Poison proofing your home is an essential step towards the safety of your pet pig. However, your pig's safety is not guaranteed and emergencies can occur at any point in time. It is good to be aware of the things and food items that can harm your pet pig and put its life in danger.

Pigs love to eat and are omnivores but that doesn't mean you can feed them anything at all. There are certain plants, vegetables and fruits that can prove to be fatal for pigs. What we as humans eat has nothing to do with what pigs eat. So make sure you do not feed your pig the leftovers from dinner and lunch.

Toxic Plants

To help pet pig owners differentiate between toxic and non-toxic foods, below is a list of plants that CANNOT be fed to a pig.

- Leaves of pigweed.
- Seeds of fiddle neck.
- Turnips.
- Broccoli.
- Cabbage.
- Mustard seeds.
- Laburnum.
- Irises.
- Tobacco.
- Golden Chain.
- Pokeweed.
- Mandrake.
- Black Cherry.
- Wild Cherry.
- Bitter Cherry.
- Choke Cherry.
- Pin Cherry.

- Bracken Fern.
- Rhubarb.
- Celery.
- Parsnip.
- Leeks.
- Cocklebur.
- Asparagus.
- Bell-peppers.
- Tea Leaves.
- Coffee Grounds.

Toxic Substances

There are certain toxic chemicals and substances that cause poisonous reactions and effects in pigs.

- Excessive Salt.
- Ammonia Gas.
- Carbon Mono-Oxide.
- Hydrogen Sulphide.
- Insecticides.
- Warfain – Rat Poison.
- Coal Tars.
- Copper.
- Iodine.
- Manganese.
- Iron.
- Zinc.
- Selenium.
- Arsenic.
- Mercury.
- Lead.
- Fluorine.
- Antibacterial Products and Medicines.

Toxic Food Items

There are several food items that cause toxicity in pigs. You cannot feed your pig anything from the refrigerator or the leftovers. Pigs are sensitive to certain elements in the food items we eat. That's why it is important for pig owners to get a copy of the list of poisonous substances that should never be fed to pigs.

- Raw Potatoes.
- Banana Peels.
- Raw Onions.
- Citrus Fruits.
- Avocados.
- Bones.
- Pumpkins.
- Algae.
- Fungus.

A pig shouldn't be fed fruits and vegetables in a great quantity as it can damage their digestive system.

Poison Proofing

Before you get your new pet home, you will need to poison proof your home. There are many things that can pose a threat to a pig's life. The things that are the most harmful for pet pigs are toxic substances such as deodorants, rubber bands, plastic, creams, anti-bacterial products, soaps, detergents, cleansers, and much more. Pig proofing your home means clearing your home of things that can be dangerous to a pig's health. You will need to:

- Dispose of food items and garbage properly.
- Garbage cans and bins should be kept in a safe place, away from the pig's reach because a garbage can contains many toxic substances that can be harmful to a pig's health.
- Put the food items in locked cabinets, out of the reach of the pig.

- Keep away rubber bands, small toys, and plastic items away from your pig's reach.
- Do not leave small items on the floor for your pig to eat.

Cleaning your home for a pig will minimize the chances of it getting hurt and injured.

Symptoms of Poisoning

If your pig has accidentally or purposely chewed upon or swallowed a toxic substance, call a rescue service or your vet immediately. When a pig ingests a poisonous substance, it will show some symptoms also known as after affects. Observe the symptoms closely as it will help your veterinary service or rescue center suggest an immediate treatment. Check the following things:

- Is the pig breathing?
- Is it seizing?
- What is its heart rate?
- Is the pig showing signs of a shock?
- Does the pig have high temperature?
- What is the color of your pig's mucous membranes?
- Is the pig hemorrhaging?
- What substance is ingested?
- The extent of exposure to toxic substance?
- When was the toxic substance ingested or when was the pig exposed to it?

Some of the common symptoms of pig poisoning are:

- Signs of bleeding under the skin.
- Symptoms of prolonged poisoning from salt and excess water include blindness, deafness, bumping into objects, aimless wandering, ear twitching, skin irritation, lack of appetite, constipation, excessive thirst, falling over side-ways, etc.

- The symptoms of poisoning from insecticides include excessive urination, vomiting, defecation, salivation, uneasiness, hind-limb paralysis, colic, etc.
- The symptoms of metal poisoning in pigs include reduced growth rate, nervous damage, and in worst cases; death.
- The symptoms of poisoning from warfarin include hematoma, bleeding from wounds, injecting sites, and rectum, excreting with blood, internal bleeding, paleness of skin due to blood loss, etc.
- The symptoms of poisoning from fungal substances in pig feed include reduced growth rate, poor metabolic rate, etc.
- The symptoms of poisoning from fungi grown in the stored summer crops include poor diet, anemia, liver damage, etc.
- A mycotoxin named Zearalenone; a female sex hormone which is fed to female pigs, usually the ones on the farms or for breeding. Feeding this substance to pigs' causes swelling and reddening of vulva, prolapsed rectum and vagina, development of the teats of gilt, and swelling of the prepuce of boars.
- A mycotoxin found in wheat causes poisonous reactions in pigs and its most prominent symptom includes lack of appetite.
- Other symptoms of poisoning in pigs include; vomits, seizures, increased heart rate, dizziness, and much more.

Treatment

When a pig is exposed to toxic substances, the first thing you need to do is get hold of your first-aid kit. After getting your first-aid kit, call the emergency rescue center or a poison control center. Tell them about your pig, its age, sex, weight, and then the signs of poisoning. After that the rescue center will give you some directions to control the effect of poison on your pig. You will then be asked to bring your pet to the center or a van will be sent over to your place.

The treatment for poisoning in pigs depends on the type of toxin it is exposed to. In some cases, an emergency first-aid kit is enough while in others, a vet or experts from the poison control center do the job. Either way, it is suggested that pig owners consult with a vet or a professional to treat their animal immediately.

- If the pig has been exposed to toxins externally, the treatment options are; ocular irrigation and bathing.
- If the pig has been exposed to toxins orally, the treatment options include; emesis, dilution, emetic agents, activated charcoal, cathartics, enemas, enterogastric lavage, and gastric lavage.
- The drugs that are commonly used to treat pig poisoning include; hydrogen peroxide, syrup of Ipecac, xylazine, activated charcoal, apomorphine, sorbitol, magnesium sulphate, and sodium sulphate.
- The drugs used to control seizures after exposure to toxins inclue; diazepam, methocarbamol, inhalant anesthetics, and barbiturates.
- Other drugs used for treatment of poisoned pet pigs include; atropine, digibind, propranolol, metoprolol, pyridoxine, flumazenil, yohimbine hydrochloride, N-acetylcysteine, ammonium chloride, furosemide, calcitonin, calcium gluconate, vitamin C, pamidronate, sodium bicarbonate, gastrointestinal protectants, physostigmine, cholestyramine, 4 MP fomepizole, vitamin K1, ethanol, pamidronate, methylene blue, phenothiazines, 2-PAM pralidoxime chloride, atropine, digibind, etc.

Animal Poison Control Centers

The first thing to do when your pig is exposed to toxic chemicals is to call your local animal poison control center. In many countries and states, an animal poison center is known as ASPCA. ASPCA is the most authentic and widely known animal rescue/poison care center that rescues millions of pets including pigs.

There are several other animal poison centers, their names and locations given below to help you get your pet treated in less time.

USA

The National Animal Poison Center at the University of Illinois

Help Line Number: 1-900-680-0000 or 1- 800-548-2423

ASPCA – American Society for the Prevention of Cruelty to Animals

Help Line Number: 1-888-4ANI-HELP (1-888-426-4435)

Pet Poison Helpline, Bloomington, USA

Help Line Number: 855-764-7661

Email: info@petpoisonhelpline.com

Fax: (952) 852-4601

Animal Poison Hotline

Help Line Number: 1-888-232-8870

Kansas State University Veterinary Teaching Hospital

Help Line Number: 1-785-532-5679

UK

Veterinary Poisons Information Center

Help Line Number: +44 (0)207 188 3314

Website: vpisglobal.com

Preventative Measures

What if your pig meets an accident and you don't know what to do?

When you buy a pig or any pet, you have to make sure that you have taken measures to protect it. Therefore, taking preventative safety measures for your pet pig is very essential. When your pet pig meets an accident in the house, sometimes you don't have the time to wait for the rescue team and have to react immediately. In such circumstances, you need to have a proper first-aid kit in your home. Moreover, a pet pig owner must know how to deal with such situations.

Pigs often get injured in homes because many owners do not set the house that suits their pigs. A pig needs to be in a house that is clear of excess stuff, furniture, slippery floors, etc. However, if these safety measures are neglected, a pig often meets an accident. Below are some tips for amateur pig owners that will keep their pigs safe in their homes.

- Is the flooring of your house pig-friendly? Or do you have slippery marble all over the place? This is the biggest hazard for a pig that walks and runs on a slippery floor. Before bringing your pet pig home, make sure that the floor of your home is non-slippery. Pigs have hooves that are hard and can slip on marbles and tiles. That's why it is best to install carpets all over the house or in the areas that your pig is going to live in. If your pig slips on the floor, it will damage its bones and might never walk again. If you want your pig to be safe, make sure you check the flooring of your home.
- If you have a lot of cabinets in your home, make a habit of closing them tightly. It is always best to keep your pig away from areas that have cabinets. Pigs are curious animals and if you leave them in a room full of cabinets, they are going to open them with help of their snouts.
- Keep hazardous chemicals and substances such as deodorants, insecticides, shampoos, etc, away from your pig. If you have

these substances and products in cabinets, do not let your pig enter the room or lock the cabinets.

- Treat your pet pig like a little child that has a curious nature.
- Do not leave your pig in a room with an electronic heater. Pigs love to stay warn in winters, especially the little ones. If they find warm objects, they stick to them to get the heat. If your pig will touch the heater, it will get burned. This also goes for refrigerators and other electronic devices.
- Another important thing to keep in mind is to keep your electric cords and wires away from the reach of your pig. Don't leave chargers plugged in, as your pig will get curious and chew on them. These plugs have electric currents and can electrocute your pig.

Prepare your home for your new pet pig. Pig-proofing your home will keep your pig safe from hazards and accidents that can be life-threatening.

12) Medicines for the Pig

When you have a pig, know that there will be accidental situations in which you will need certain medicines and items to provide immediate medical support to your pig. Sometimes a pig gets injured and due to lack of medical supplies, the pig suffers through prolonged infection and illness. To avoid situations like these, pig owners should always have a medicine kit on hand.

Buy a box or bag for your pig to keep its medical supplies and drugs in it. The medicines you will need in the bag for emergency situations include:

- Aspirin.
- Distilled water.
- Hydrogen peroxide.
- Cranberry juice Pedialyte.
- Gatorade.
- Antibiotic ointment.
- Vaseline.

- Baytril.
- Neosporin.
- Tylan.
- Penicillin G.
- Betadine.
- Pepto Bismol.
- Electrolytes.
- Mylanta.
- Benadryl.
- Antihistamine.
- Spectomycin.
- SMZ.

Medicines used in case of an injury or accident are a must for your pig's medical kit. Moreover, keep antibiotics in your kit, which you can ask your vet to prescribe.

Pigs are curious, they love to play, and are escape artists. That's why it is very common for a pig to fall or get injured. These injuries can sometimes become a greater problem if not dealt with immediately. Having a medicinal kit will allow pet pig owners to keep their pigs safe from major infections and injuries.

13) Giving Medicine to the Pig

It is not so difficult to make your pig eat medicine. Pigs are active eaters and are fond of chewing on food pieces and other items they find on the ground. When a pig is sick or injured, owners can add their pill or medicine with the food. Another way is to crush the tablet in cranberry juice or add it in its meal. The pig will create no troubles in eating the food without noticing the medicine.

14) Physical Exercise

Before bringing your pet pig into your home, you will need to conduct a little research on the type of environment that the pigs need to stay healthy and fit. You will need to adjust your home in such a way that your pig gets proper space that it can play in and get its daily dose of physical exercise.

Pigs love food and no matter what size or age you get it, it will soon grow into a fatty. Their weight is what makes it essential for them to exercise regularly. You will need to create an outdoor area for your pig to run around and play. This will not only help it stay healthy but it will also boost up its mood.

Space

The most important thing for a pig is to have enough space to play. The indoor space of your home will not be enough for your pig as it will need a larger area, preferably a garden or a ground. Create an area outside your home and fence it up. do not use lousy fences because pigs love to escape and they are strong animals that can easily break fences.

If you do not have an outdoor space, you can give your pig an empty room. It is very essential for a pig's health to walk and stay physically active.

Walk

The best way to keep your pig healthy through physical activity is walking it in the morning. Of course you will need to take walking rights for your pig and once you get approved, you can take your pig on morning walks. This is the best way to ensure that the pig has some physical activity. Pigs are naturally very active animals. They like to walk, run and play. They need proper mental and physical exercise daily. Walking will help protect your pig from different diseases including obesity and much more.

A pig's nature is very similar to that of a dog. They are the best companions and love to walk. Make sure you have your pig's harness on before you take it to a walk in public places. Firstly, you will need to train your pet pig to behave in public areas. You will also need to harness train it so that it feels comfortable with it. Once your pig has learned to behave, you can take it for a walk. Regular walks are also good for hooves trimming.

Exploring

Another way that owners can include physical exercise at home is by letting their pig explore its surroundings. It is best to provide a clear area or room to your pig and have toys around so that it stays distracted. Do not leave your pig in a room without toys as it will get bored and become destructive. Have some newspapers, cardboards and fluffy toys around and your pig will enjoy its time.

Dirt Box

Let your pig root. Rooting is a pig's favorite hobby that you cannot get rid of. If you don't want your pig to ruin your yard, make sure you provide it with a dirt pool of its own. Their natural instinct can kick in anytime and a dirt pool will not only keep your pig happy but it will also provide adequate physical exercise. You can make this more interesting for your pet pig by adding pebbles and small rocks inside its dirt box. Hide little treats in the box so that your pig struggles to get it out. If you don't want to leave your pet outside for any reason, create a rooting game for it in its room. Gather towels and blankets and hide treats in them. This will be very similar to rooting, giving your pig a good physical exercise.

Daily Exercise Routine

To keep track of your pig's daily physical exercise, you will need to design an exercise routine for it. Think of activities that will provide proper physical and mental exercise for your pig.

- Playtime – introduce a play time for your pet pig but avoid feeding it to many treats as it will only increase its weight. The play time cannot be boring as your pig will easily get distracted and aggressive if bored. Set-up a rooting box full of blankets and hide your pig's favorite toy in it.

- Place your pig's food, litter and bedding far from one another. This will give your pig a little walk every time it wants to poo, eat or sleep.
- Set a time for your pig's walk outdoors with a harness on. Do not change timings everyday as it will disturb the pig.
- You can also set up pool for your pig so that it swims in it and have fun at the same time.

Play-time

If you get bored while walking your pig or letting it outdoors, try to engage it in a game. Designate a time of the day for your pig's play-time and choose a fun game to play. This will not only keep you entertained but will also help the pig stay in a good mood. Play-time games include; hiding your pig's favorite toy under the mud, hiding chunks of treat in your pig's bed, hide n seek, and much more. Try to think of new games for your pig that will be much more entertaining than the usual walk.

15) Micro-Chipping and Tattooing

Every day we hear about a pet getting lost and their owners not able to find them. Micro-chipping and tattooing is for the safety of the pets. Pigs are natural escapers and no matter how hard you try to stop them, they will escape. That's why it becomes extremely important for pet pigs to get micro-chipped or tattooed.

What is Micro-Chipping?

A micro-chip is an electronic identification for a pet. It is the size of a grain of rice and is inserted under the skin, between the shoulders blades at the back of your pig. This micro-chip has a scanner which detects the location of a pet. There is a database where the microchips are present with their number and the pet and the owner's contact information. So, in case your pet pig gets lost, you can track its location with help of a micro-chip.

Make sure you keep the contact information on the database updated so that your pet could be tracked if lost. If you have bought a new pet pig, make sure you change the contact details on its micro-chip number.

Micro-chipping is not a painful process as the micro-chip is the size of a rice grain. It is placed under the skin using a syringe and only a little discomfort can be felt which pets usually forget in a little while.

The right time to get your pet pig micro-chipped is when you buy it from a shelter or a pet shop. You will first need to consult with your vet regarding micro-chipping and then get it done. To get your pig micro-chipped, it is important that you visit an authorized micro-chip implanter.

What is Tattooing?

Tattooing serves a similar purpose as a micro-chip. It is meant to identify a pet, its owner, breed, etc. Tattooing a pig in the ear or its butt muscle is a mark of identification that mostly farm pigs get. Tattooing is one of the ways animal and humane societies mark animals.

To get your pet pig tattooed, you can contact your vet and ask for different tattoo artists for pets. Make sure you opt for a licensed tattoo artist for the safety of your pet. A tattoo artist will use an engraving pen to write your pet's name, your identification number and whatever info you need to put on it. a tattoo is also very helpful in finding a lost pet. Tattooing in pets usually involves a code that is engraved into the skin of the animal. This unique code is registered with the animal society of that particular country. The code is saved in the database with the owner's contact details in case you don't want to tattoo a lot of things on your pet pig. You will also need to fill out paper-work for registering your pet.

The process of tattooing is not very painful either. However, you need to make sure that your pig feels comfortable. Pigs can get little tough when they are forced to do something. Make your pet pig comfortable around the environment, offer it treats, and rub its belly if needed. Only then you will be able to get a tattoo on its skin.

Choose the Best Option

Tattooing or micro-chipping, which one's the best option?

Before planning on getting your pet registered with the shelters and animal societies, make sure you do your research. You will need to talk to pet owners, animal societies or simply search the Internet to find out the best procedure for the identification of your pet.

However, micro-chipping is more authentic than tattooing as the identity of a pet and its owner are saved in a database and from there the pet is electronically tracked down. There have been cases when pets have been stolen and the tattoo was removed with ink. That's why pig owners are suggested to look for the best option available for the identification of their pet. It is always best to adopt preventative measures with your pet pigs as they are cunning escapers. Enrolling your pet pig in the database gives owners a greater chance of getting reunited with their pigs.

16) Licensing

If you have a pet pig, dog or cat, you will need to get it licensed. Every pet that comes in this world needs to get licensed by a state's law. Unlicensed pets are usually picked up by the pound and in places where the laws are strict, many unlicensed pets get terminated.

Every country has different policies and rules against pet pigs. Some countries have strict rules for animal populations and to control the growing population, they terminate unlicensed or homeless pets. So, if you don't want your pet to be taken away, make sure you get it licensed.

Reasons to License Your Pet Pig Today!

There are several reasons to get your pet pig licensed.

- In many countries, it is a law to get pet pigs licensed.
- If you don't get your pig licensed and get caught, you will be charged with a great fine.
- A licensed pig is easier to locate in case it gets lost.
- Licensed pigs that are lost will get support from rescue centers and pet shelters all over the country.
- Licensed pigs have a better chance at getting adopted or bought.
- Unlicensed pigs are the first ones to get euthanized.
- If you are caught with an unlicensed pig, you will be charged an amount of $250 in the US - £165 in UK.
- The fee for licensing your pig is far less as compared to the penalty of an unlicensed pet.
- A licensed pig is one which is up-to-date on its vaccination.
- Licensing your pet means that the pet is healthy.
- The fee of licensing your pet pig goes to different animal shelters in your country that is helpful in feeding other pet animals.
- The licensing fee is as little as $20 in the US or £20 in UK.

How to Get a License?

Due to the growing reputation of licensed animals, many countries have made licensing offices available in different regions and communities. Many licensing counties have their website that allows licensing through the mail. If your pet pig is already licensed, make sure you get its license renewed every year.

What Will You Need?

To get your pet pig licensed under your city or state, you will need:

- Your pig should be 4 months or older.
- To get a license, you will need to show documents of your pig's health including the vaccinations it has had.
- In case you move to another country, you will need to re-license your pig with that city's licensing department.

17) Pet Insurance

Pet care and safety has become an essential part of today's world. Millions of people are spending a lot of money every year on vets and animal medication. The main reason behind these peaked bills is the advancement of technology and drugs. There were times when animals did not get proper medical aid and there were diseases that were tagged as fatal. However, with the development in animal medicine and equipment, pet owners are not able to keep their pets safe from a variety of illnesses which increases the chance of their survival.

If you go to the vet to get your pig groomed or vaccinated, you will be charged with a hefty amount. Veterinary bills are not the only thing that you have to look after. That's why many banks have introduced pet insurance.

Should You Get It?

The question that many pet pig owners ask is: should they get a pet insurance?

If you want to secure your pig's future, it is best to get pet insurance. Pet insurance is really helpful as it saves a lot of money. People that have pet insurance feel less burdened and feel safe from emergency situations.

Benefits of Getting a Pet Insurance

To help pig owners decide, below is a list of benefits you can enjoy after getting pet insurance.

- Getting pet insurance will help you pay for emergency bills in case of an accident or an injury.
- Pet insurance will cost you as much as $50 a month in the US - £29 in UK.
- Pet insurance helps you save thousands of dollars.
- Pet insurance will help you save out-of-pocket expenditures.
- Pet insurance will provide your pet with a better chance at living a healthy life.
- What if you don't have enough cash in hand when your pig is in an accident? In these cases, a pet insurance helps owners get their pet operated immediately.
- Pet insurance covers a lot of expenses of your pig's care and vet's visits.
- If your pet pig has a severe illness, a pet insurance will help you cover lifelong expenses for its treatment.

Types of Pet Insurance

Every bank has different packages for pet insurance. Some cover a variety of expenses while others are cheaper. The most common type of pet insurance includes:

- Accident Only – in this type of insurance cover, you can get your pet operated or treated after an accident. Some banks also have a time and money limit. This cover doesn't include the treatment of illnesses.
- Per Condition with a Time Limit – this type of insurance is very affordable as it covers the cost of visits to the vet for any operation and illness. However, it has a time limit to it and the bills are only covered for 12 months after an illness has been diagnosed. When the bill exceeds the insurance amount, many banks charge more to cover it.
- Per Condition, No Time Limit – in this type of insurance, a bank will ask for a fixed fee that will cover the cost of treatments to illnesses and injuries. There is no time limit to this cover and the renewal of this cover should be done every 12 months. This insurance does not cover re-occurring illnesses and injuries.

- Lifetime – lifetime cover for pet insurance is the most widespread cover and the most expensive one. This type of cover is best for all types of medical bills, vet bills, treatment bills, injury bills, pregnancy bills, burial bills, and much more. The insurer usually charges a high amount per year but covers almost every type of bill related to your pet. This cover also includes prepared treatments like vaccinations etc.

Always compare different insurances before buying one. Some insurance offers are better than other. Do not get fooled or rigged by banks that attract by advertising cheap insurance fee.

18) Where to get Pet Insurance?

A few years back, it was hard to find a good pig insurance provider because pigs weren't popular as pets. However, nowadays there are several pet insurance providers that can easily be found on the Internet.

Do a thorough search and make sure to compare several insurance companies re prices and terms.

Chapter 13: Financial Aspects

There is a cost that comes with a pet. When you adopt or buy a pig, there will be certain costs that you will need to keep in mind. It is always best to consider the financial requirements and then finalize the decision of bringing a pet pig home. Getting a pig as pet is a huge responsibility because the pig will need a lot of care and maintenance. Just like humans spend money on a new family member, they need to spend a lot on pets too. Your pet pigs will need the basic care at your home including proper shelter, food, grooming, cleaning, medical care and much more. If you plan things ahead, it becomes easier to calculate the finances and prepare to deal with them in an organized manner. Apart from the initial costs of getting a pig, there are additional costs associated with it.

1) Food

Your pet pig might gain up to 100 pounds and that simply means that you will need to spend a lot on pig feed. Pigs are foodies and they will need to be fed twice a day. It is best to buy pet pig feed from the market. Do not buy food meant for farm hogs as their diet includes a lot of protein which can be harmful for your pet pig. Feed two bowls of food to your pet pig to keep it safe from obesity. An adult pig can consume 1- 12lbs grain in a day. Your pig feed will cost you around $1000 a year - £660.

2) Accessories

Accessories for pigs can include a vast variety of things from its harness to jewels. Buying accessories for your pig will cost you a lot of money as it is listed under luxury. The essential accessories that you will need to buy include; harness, leash, bedding, blanket, sweaters, food bowls, shampoo, soap, etc. There are other grooming accessories that you will need including a trimmer for hooves, Q-tips for ears, skin lotion for your pig's sensitive skin. There are some local pet stores that offer accessories at affordable rates and have great packages and sales.

3) The Vet

The greatest cost that owners will incur will be the cost of the vet. Every time a pig owner visits a vet, whether for hooves trimming or a vaccine, he/she will be charged. An owner will be spending a lot of money on the vet and medical bills. Due to the advancement in technology and medicine, the costs of medicine and visits to the vet have become very expensive. Before brining a pet pig home, one must consider the costs of the vet. Moreover, there will be times when your pig will need superior care in case of an emergency or accident. These costs will multiply in such circumstances. An average person cannot afford the cost of the vet and usually end up giving away their pet pigs. To avoid such events, one must take pet insurance into consideration. Many insurers provide coverage for medical bills, visit to the vet, operations, treatment to illnesses and much more. Getting a pet insurance simply provides you financial support when you need it.

4) Training

Training your pet pig is not as expensive as other things. Training simply means that you will need to invest your time into teaching your pet good habits and tricks. Although, during the training process you will need to offer treats to your pig. These treats will be in the form of small food items. You will need to take care of the amount of treats you feed your pig. Offer only a few treats when teaching your pig to learn good manners. If you over-feed your pigs, they will get really fat.

5) Miscellaneous Expenses

There are some other things that will cost you some money including neutering and spaying, micro-chipping and tattooing, pet insurance, pet licensing, travelling your pet pig, registering your pet pig, etc. Always stay prepared to spend a little extra on our pet pig to keep it healthy and happy.

Chapter 14: Luxurious Pet Pig Grooming

Some people love to give a whole new meaning to pig grooming. Apart from showers, hooves trimming, etc, many people like to dress them up. A recent trend in pig petting shows that people that are buying tea-cup pigs are making them wear costumes and nail colors. Some of them have been seen wearing glasses, jewels and hats too.

Many rescue centers and pet shelters are organizing fun events for pigs in which they dress them up for parties and much more. The entire concept of dressing a pig up is to spread a positive word about them. Many people are still afraid of pigs and do not consider them as pet animals. To change this misconception about such loving animals, many people are trying to groom them so that people could see the good side of these animals.

1) Dress Them Up!

People love to dress-up miniature pigs because of their tiny stature. Moreover, tea-cup pigs are extremely adorable. The trend of buying miniature pigs emerged when famous celebrities adopted pigs. Since then, people have started to like pigs and have made them their choice of pet.

A good time pass with mini pets is dressing them up. You can choose mini pig clothes, frocks, hoodies, sweaters, boots, hats, jewels, coats, etc, and dress it up for a piggy party. This is a good way to bond with your little pal, as it will feel happy being around you. Not to forget that your mini pigs will look extremely adorable in tiny outfits and ready to drop jaws.

2) Fancy Pig Accessories

There are several stores, online and offline, that offer fancy pig accessories. These accessories are listed under luxury items and can be very expensive. Some of the most common pig accessories available in the stores are:

- Hats
- Nail Paints
- Scarves
- Jackets
- Coats
- Sweaters
- Bracelets
- Jewelry
- Handbags
- Tiara
- Bandanna
- Boots
- Umbrella
- Raincoat
- Sun Glasses
- Necklace
- Frocks
- Gowns
- Ribbons
- Tie
- Socks
- Costumes
- Bows

Chapter 15: General Tips, Tricks and Guidelines

Having a pet pig at home gets really tough if you have little or no experience with them. There are certain areas where pig owners go wrong. If you think you have petted a dog and you can handle a pig, you are wrong. Pig is a different animal that has different needs and natural instincts. Before you choose to get a pig, make sure you have learnt all about the animal.

Pigs are known for their loving nature and we also hear a lot about their aggression. It is common for pigs to get upset and charge at their owners as well. To avoid bad behaviors like these, pig owners must know how to deal with them effectively.

Pigs are naturally curious and extremely intelligent animals. This combination can sometimes prove to be lethal for pet pig owners. If you are thinking of keeping pigs as pets, make sure you have learnt all about their behavior, attitude, mood swings, positive and negative sides, and much more.

1) Handle Baby Pigs with Care

If you have bought a baby pig, do not follow the instruction for an adult pig. Piglets are different from adult pigs and more fragile. They will need intensive care and endless love so that they become comfortable in a new place. Some people find it easy to pet baby pigs as they are not harmless and don't have aggression problems. However, piglet owners should be aware that small pigs need aggressive care.

A baby pig doesn't know how to eat food or drink water. That's where the job for the owner becomes tough. Apart from food, a baby pig's living area is very different from that of an adult pig. A baby pig should live in a playpen. They should not be left in open spaces or rooms where they can pick up little things from the floor and chew them up. There are other safety hazards for little pigs as they are tiny and cannot handle injuries.

Petting a baby pig is a huge responsibility and the owner needs to realize that. Piglets do not generate their own body heat, which means they will need to be kept in a warm place. The ideal temperature for a baby pig is 90 degrees. Any temperature below that will cause an illness and immediate death. Baby piglets will need to be kept above heating pads and wrapped with comfy blankets so that they stay warm.

Do not turn on the AC if you have are sharing your room with a piglet. Pigs are extremely sensitive to temperatures, especially the little ones. If your baby pigs catches a cold, it is likely to die from it and that's the reason most of the piglets don't survive with owners.

Another mistake that baby pig owners make is giving dangerous toys to it. Do not buy pointy and hard toys for your piglet. A piglet will be safe playing with soft stuffed toys.

Do not over feed your piglet as its stomach and digestive system is not fully developed. Mother pigs only feed its babies 4 times a day. Feeding a lot of milk to your piglet will cause diarrhea which is fatal for the little ones.

Do not feed a lot of food items to your piglet as it will be hard for it to digest. Keep your piglet on goat's milk and rice cereal till the age of 3 weeks.

It is better to buy a pig older than 8 months to reduce the risk of losing it. It is very tough to take care and nurture a baby pig.

2) The Warning Signs

Pigs are friendly, social, and affectionate animals. They usually don't act-up with their owners but we often hear stories of pet pig owners getting hurt by their pigs. So how does this happen? How does a pig hurt its owner?

There are many factors that contribute to a pig's bad behavior and aggression. One of the biggest problems pig owners face is getting bit by their pig. Pigs are omnivores and that's why they can eat both meat and vegetables. So, if you feed them food with your fingers, you are likely to get bit or lose your finger.

While training your pet pig, you will need to feed it in a flat bowl instead of feeding it with your hands. Be cautious and attentive when dealing with pigs. However, if you treat your pig the right way, there will hardly be any accidents or incidents.

3) Helping Your Pet Pig Transition

Pet pig owners or any other pet owners for the matter of fact face a hard time when they are being given an option of euthanizing their pet. Letting a loved one go away forever is indeed a hard decision to make. However, it is for the best of their pet.

Euthanasia means putting a living being to sleep that is suffering from an incurable disease or illness. The process is painless and meant to take the pet out of massive stress and pain.

It might be difficult to tell the vet to euthanize your pet pig that you dearly love, but in some cases, it becomes absolutely necessary to do so. It is a psychologically difficult time for pet owners. However, the families that are given proper knowledge about the process and its purpose feel better about making this tough decision.

Euthanasia – What, Why and How?

Euthanasia in pet pigs means giving a painless death to a pig with an incurable illness that is causing it a lot of pain and anxiety.

Pet owners at some point will need to face this sad reality and they should be prepared for it when they buy a pet. It is essential to know that euthanasia is for the betterment of their pet and themselves too. When a pet pig is sick and diagnosed with an incurable disease, their owners take them to vet and ask for the cure. The vet will try and conduct different procedures on the poor soul. The owners will have to go through a prolonged period of stress that will cause disturbance in their life. Trying to treat your pig of a condition that is incurable will only lead to your pig getting hurt, you spending thousands of dollars on medical bills, and suffering from emotional stress.

Many pig owners and families start to feel bad and blame themselves for not doing something too soon. This is the wrong approach and will only hurt you more.

Complete Guide for Pig Owners

When your vet tells you that your pig needs to be euthanized and that there is no hope left, you feel extremely stressed. That's why it is important for pig owners to have complete information of the process and only let them make a decision once they are totally comfortable with it and its benefits to their pet.

Is Euthanasia Painful?

The biggest concern for pet pig owners is whether or not this procedure is painful for their pets.

It is important that your vet tell you all about euthanasia. The first thing that most pig owners want to hear is that their pet is not going to feel any pain. The vet needs to tell the owners that their pig is under mental and physical stress. It is extremely essential for pet pig owners to learn that their pig is suffering through a lot of pain and anxiety. This will make them make a decision quicker, without making their pet suffer more.

Anxiety for Pigs

The first thing that a vet should tell the pig owner is the anxiety that their pet pig is going through. Pigs are omnivores and Mother Nature has made them the prey, that's why they feel threatened when they are sick. They know that they will become somebody else's food. This thought haunts them and they feel stressed. Apart from this stress, they will feel very low because of their illness. Pigs are active animals and like to walk, play and run. So, when a pig gets sick, it is not able to perform with its complete strength, which makes it extremely sad and depressed.

To get a clearer idea of how your pet feels when you take it to the vet, think about the times you took it for different procedures. Was your pet feeling comfortable in the operating room? Was it looking at you with innocent eyes? Was your pig feeling hopeless?

Pigs do not feel comfortable at the vet and that's why when owners take them for operations, they feel anxiety. Just as anxiety is bad for humans, it does the same to pigs. Before the actual illness kills your pet pig, the anxiety will.

Pain for Pigs

The physical trauma that a pig goes through when you take it to the vet for a variety of procedures is beyond imagination. Just because your pet pig can't speak, doesn't mean it wants to go through all of it. The procedure of euthanasia is not painful at all but making the pig suffer for a longer time is. The pain that is attached to an illness can become life threatening. The organs and systems gradually stop working, the pig doesn't consume any food, it keeps on throwing up, and can't move a muscle. In such cases, a pig is going through the worst kind of pain by staying alive. So, the best option is to euthanize it and ease its pain with a painless procedure.

When to know that Your Pig Needs to be Euthanized?

It is not always a bad news if your pet pig is suffering from a disease. Sometimes owners get the good news that their pet's condition can be treated. However, the chance of getting a treatment option for your pig is very low. It is essential for the owners to learn everything about euthanasia if their pet pig is suffering from a fatal health condition.

There are certain factors that approve your pet pig for euthanasia. Read on to the list below to find out if your pig needs to be euthanized.

- If your adult pet pig is not accepting any food for 5 – 7 days, it needs to be euthanized.
- If your piglet is not accepting food for 1 – 3 days.
- If your pet pig gets an infection in any of its organs and the anti-biotic stops working.
- If your pig loses 25% of its body weight due to an illness.
- If your pig is not able to stand on its own and seems very weak.
- If an organ or system of your pig fails to work or develops a problem.
- If your pig has excess blood loss.
- If your pig is suffering from a respiratory illness like cyanosis or dyspnea.
- If your pet pig has severe dehydration, vomiting, diarrhea.
- If your pig is gone in depression.
- If your pig is having seizures or paralysis.
- If your pig has a renal failure.
- If your pig has extensive muscle damage.
- If your pig has a severe bone injury that can't be operated.
- If your pig has untreatable wounds.

These are the reasons that will give you a better idea of what to do. You can get information and details on euthanasia from your vet on the condition of your pig. Before making the final decision, make sure you are absolutely satisfied with the procedure.

The Process of Euthanizing a Pig

There are different methods of euthanizing a pet pig. These methods depend upon the age, size, weight, and condition of the animal. The methods adopted to euthanize piglets are different from that of adult pigs. That's why every pig owner should choose the best method of euthanizing their pig.

The Right Ways

Euthanizing a beloved pet pig is a tough decision but to ensure that your pig leaves this world in peace, you will need to learn about the right and painless methods of euthanizing. Do not let your pet suffer for a long period of time. Instead, choose to euthanize when there is no hope left for it.

1. Injecting Barbiturate Drug

The most common method used to euthanize small pigs is by injecting barbiturate intravenously. Barbiturate is a drug that is very similar to pig anesthetic that vets use during operations. The dose injected directly into the vein is high in quantity which puts the pet to sleep without causing discomfort or pain. Barbiturate drug comes in different names including pentobarbitone, valabarb, lethabarb, and pentobarb. This drug is a green liquid, which makes it easier to be identified. Barbiturate enters the blood stream and makes its heart and brain stop. This method of euthanizing a pig is widely adopted, as the animal dies a peaceful death. Injecting a very high dose of barbiturate drug can sometimes cause discomfort and pain to the pig. That's why it is extremely essential that you opt for an experienced vet to do the job.

2. Injecting Potassium Chloride

Another method used for euthanizing a pet pig is by injecting potassium chloride intravenously. The potassium chloride that enters the blood streams causes the potassium level to rise in the blood. When the potassium level rises, it causes heart arrhythmia. Potassium chloride injection is painful, that's why vets and experts are not suggested to inject it without using anesthesia. Anesthesia causes the pig to go to sleep which makes it painless for the pet. This method is very similar to injecting barbiturate into the bloodstream.

137

3. Intravenous Injection of Sodium Pentobarbital

Sodium pentobarbital is a sedating drug used for animal euthanasia. This is the suggested way of euthanizing a pet pig, as it is not painful at all. Many countries have different laws against the methods of euthanasia for pets. Pet pigs should be euthanized using the correct or prescribed dosage of sodium pentobarbital.

The Wrong Ways

There are certain methods listed under euthanasia that might cause pain to your pig. That's why it is important to know what ways can harm your pig.

1. Gassing

Gassing is a method that is not used to euthanize pet animals including pigs. Some animals are euthanized using carbon dioxide and carbon monoxide but pet pigs aren't. Gassing is considered equivalent to slaughtering a pet. Other gassing methods include usage of Nitrous oxide and halothane gases. These gasses cause irritation in pigs and become very painful. Pigs that are gassed struggle inside the box to get air. The pig slowly suffocates and dies a painful death. This method of euthanizing a pet pig is not approved by many countries and animal welfare organizations around the world. The main purpose of euthanizing a pet is to ease it from the pain of a disease etc. However, this painful process only makes things worse for the animal.

2. Electrocution

Electrocution is another method of putting an animal to sleep but a rather violent one. Electrocuting pigs for euthanasia is not allowed and pig owners must be aware of it. Never listen to anyone that gives you an idea of electrocuting your pet pig because the process is very painful for the pet.

3. Cervical Dislocation

Cervical dislocation means breaking the neck of a pet and is termed as a humane way of putting an animal to sleep. This method is not used with big pigs and can only be performed on piglets.

4. Captive Bolt Euthanasia

Another humane way of euthanizing a pig is through a captive bolt. The animal is shot with a gun that fires a steel bar/bolt at high-speed and with intense force. The increased speed and force makes this process painless and quick. This method of euthanizing is carried out by professionals that are certified to do so. These professionals know where to hit the bolt. The bolt is hit on the front of the head which directly hits the area of the brain that causes sudden death. The major cause of death in this method is caused by catastrophic injury to the brain.

Natural Death Vs Euthanasia

When your pet pig is suffering from a fatal illness or disease, you are told to get it euthanized. Euthanizing is the best option to ease your pet from immense pain but at the same time it is a crucial decision, especially for owners.

There have been cases in which a sick pig died in its sleep. This is called a true 'peaceful sleep'. However, not everyone is as lucky. That's why when pig owners feel helpless for their pig; they usually consider the option of natural death. The reason behind it is that they fail to realize that natural death is sudden and can't be estimated. Waiting for natural death to occur will take a lot of time and will only prolong your pet pig's suffering, pain and anxiety.

So, if your pet pig gets sick and cannot be treated, make sure you choose to euthanize it. Euthanizing using the right method will be absolutely painless for your pet. Before you decide, take time to do your research about pet pig euthanasia. Your local shelter or vet will give you details on the best method available. However, do not leave it all on your vet and look up the Internet to find authentic information. This way you might save your pet pig from getting euthanized using the wrong method.

Declaring Death

After the pig is euthanized, the next step is to determine whether the procedure worked or not. This is usually done by your vet's staff or an authorized personnel's team. The pig will be monitored until death has been confirmed. To confirm the pig's death, the staff will:

- Check for corneal reflexes. This is done by touching the eyeballs of the pig and if the pig doesn't blink, it is dead.
- Check its response to stimulus which means that the staff will prick the pig's nose with a pin and if the pig doesn't react, it means it is dead.
- Check the heartbeat of the pig.
- Check the breathing activity.
- Check the muscle movement.

Once the staff has confirmed no response from the pig, it is declared dead.

General Tips

Euthanasia might seem a simple procedure when done by an expert. However, it can go horribly wrong. There should be preventative measures taken before the actual process.

- Do not choose a method that will put the staff or the animal in danger.
- Use precautions before using any equipment for euthanasia.
- The staff that will perform euthanasia should wear safety suits.
- Do not make the pig aggressive or aware of what is going to happen.

- Make sure that the staff makes your pet pig feel comfortable or else it might end up in someone getting hurt.
- Opt for professionals that have experience performing euthanasia for pet pigs.
- Opt for a professional that causes least pain to your pig.
- A successful euthanasia is the one in which the pig loses its consciousness within seconds.
- Stay away from two-step process of euthanizing your pig.

4) Where Most Pet Owners Go Wrong

There are certain things that one must avoid with pet pigs. People that are new to keeping pigs as pets will face a lot of trouble with their pigs. With time, they will realize that their behavior and attitude towards their pig has made it stubborn, aggressive, and violent. To help pet pig owners around the world, below is a list of things you should avoid and adopt.

Experimentation

Pigs have specific needs and wants that every pig owner should know about. It is not healthy to experiment with your pet pig without knowing all about its nature, health concerns, moods and much more. Many pet owners make a huge mistake of treating pigs like other conventional pets. Below is a list of things that you shouldn't experiment with your pet pig.

- Do not offer your food to your pig as many ingredients and components of human food are harmful for pigs.
- Do not feed cat or dog food to your pig as it is high in protein content that is harmful for the health of pigs.
- Do not let your pig graze inside the house as it will chew on little things o n the floor.
- Do not feed fruits in great quantity.
- Do not over feed your pig by giving it food thrice or four times a day.
- Do not leave your pig alone in the outdoors or in the open.
- Do not hand feed your pig as it will be dangerous for you.

Sleeping in Your Bed

Many a times, pig owners make little mistakes out of love that prove to be very costly in the future. When you bring a small pig home, you would want to treat it nicely so that it adjusts quickly in its new home.

The biggest mistake is to let your pig sleep with you in the bed. Mini-pigs is a name given to pigs so that they sell but in reality, these pigs grow into big fat animals that are harder to control. If you think that you can handle a little pig in your bed, you are not aware of the full-grown size of a pig. Once your pig will grow into an adult, it will become a problem for you.

Letting your pig sleep in your bed will make the pig feel that the bed belongs to it. So, when you will try to get it off or change its habit, it will show aggression, and in worst cases, become violent towards you. That's why it is important for pig owners to learn that pigs should have their own beds to sleep in.

Playing Too Hard or Too Long

Of course pigs love to play and socialize. However, pigs do get irritated and bored. Many pig owners make a mistake of going over-board with their pig. This often happens when the owner is trying to train their pet pig. Pigs are generally well-behaved and will not act-up unless they are extremely irritated, bored, angry, and hungry.

Playing for long hours with your pig will make it aggressive. Just like humans have a limit, pigs do too. They will not react well to prolonged training sessions or playtimes. Once your pig is showing signs that it has had enough, end the training session by giving it a reward so that it calms down.

Hand Play

As humans, we love to make physical contact with our pet animals. People who have previously owned dogs and cats treat pigs in a similar way as well. This is where owners go wrong.

Unlike your dog and cat, pigs are not carnivores. They can eat both; herbs and meat. So, feeding them with your hands is not a good option. This is a mistake that could cost them their hand or finger. Sometimes people use hand play with their pigs. This is the same as feeding a pig with your hands.

If you want to avoid un-necessary injuries, make sure you are not using your hand to feed or play with your pig.

Extraordinary Creation

Many people get excited when they buy a pig. They start to recreate the space and design its room. Designing an extra-ordinary place for your pig is not a very good idea. Of course your pig has some needs that should be fulfilled by you but do not overdo things. Decorating the pig's room and stuffing it with furniture, etc, should be avoided.

Your pig will need a clear space, a comfy bed, a litter box, a mud pool, and clean water and food bowls. Anything other than these necessary items will cause problems for you and your pig. So, when you see your décor going down, don't be so surprised.

Pet pig owners should hazard-proof their homes before getting a pig because pigs ten to get destructive. They will ruin the furniture, household, etc.

Being Too Distracted

During the training process of your pet pig, make sure you train it with complete focus. Similarly, it is also important that the pig is not too distracted with the things in its surroundings.

Pigs get easily distracted; make sure there's nothing too interesting in its surrounding when you are trying to train it. Don't train it in front of other people. Do not keep food where you are training your pig. A distracted pig is less likely to learn anything.

No Need for Training

'I got a pig from an amazing pet store and I don't need to train it.'

'I bought my pet pig from a family. It must be trained, so I'll not invest time in training it all over again.'

These are some common dialogues we hear from new pet pig owners. When you buy a pig, it is extremely essential to train it in its initial days. No matter how well it had been trained by its previous owner, you will need to make it learn your rules and commands.

There might be instances in which a pig that has been bought from a family will become aggressive. Pigs are like dogs; loyal. So, when these pigs are forced to change homes, they go under depression which shows in their attitude and behavior. That's why it is important to train your pig whether it is previously trained or not.

A pig that isn't trained creates a lot of problems for its owners. It shows aggression when it is asked to stop, it becomes violent when it is denied of something, and much more. These are the tantrums that go away with training. If you will not train your pig, you will soon realize that it was a bad decision. Start training your pet pig as soon as it becomes comfortable with you.

Inconsistent Orders

Consistency is the key for training a pig. If you will change your commands and orders all the time, your pig will face a hard time learning anything at all. Consistent training is one thing which does not create confusions for your pet pig.

For example: if your pig is used to sleeping in beds, do not start getting irritated at this behavior. This will create confusions in your pig's head as it will have trouble discriminating between right and wrong.

Many pig owners ruin the entire training process by giving inconsistent orders. Make sure you involve other family members in the training process. Sometimes when there are several people living together, they give out different orders, instructions, and commands to the pig. These mixed commands, reactions, and orders confuse your pig and as a result it doesn't learn anything at all.

Not Using Enough Treats

It is wrong to offer too many treats during the training process of your pet pig because it can create health problems. However, giving too little can also become a trouble.

Treats are offered to a pig when it obeys a command, learns a trick, and behaves well. If you limit the quantity of treats, your pig is not going to take it too well. When you don't offer a treat when your pig follows your command, you will make it aggressive. Pigs become destructive when they don't get a treat when they are expecting one. In many cases, pigs have charged at owners when they didn't get a treat. So, make sure you have treats available at all times. Keep your pig happy and enjoy an irreplaceable bond with it.

Leaving It off the Leash

It is very essential to train your pig to wear a harness and a leash. Many experts, pig trainers, and vets suggest that pig owners start leash training in the initial days. There will be times when you will need to take your pig for a walk or out in the open. However, if you fail to leash train your pig, you will either see it running away or getting extremely uncomfortable.

The purpose of leash training is to control the activity and actions of your pig. Pigs are strong animals and weigh a lot. There is no way that you will be able to stop a 400 pound animal on your own. There are numerous benefits of leash training your pig.

- A pig that is leach trained can go on outings with the whole family.
- A leash trained pig can travel safely.
- A leash trained pig isn't harmful to others.
- A leash trained pig can be taken outdoors including family parks.
- A leash trained pig is well-behaved and easily visits the vet.
- A leash trained pig will walk at your desired pace.

Leaving it Unattended

Leaving your pig un-attended is a big NO-NO. Pigs are social animals and that's why they will need people around them. A mistake that most pig owners make is leaving their pigs all by themselves. When pigs are left alone, they become depressed and bored. This depression triggers their aggressive behavior and they lose their temper.

A pig that is angry can be very destructive. It will not only hurt itself but the things around it including furniture, floor, windows, and much more. So, don't be astonished if you find your home turned upside down.

Expecting too much!

No matter how friendly or sociable your pet pig is, never expect too much from it. Many pig owners make a mistake of expecting too much form their pigs. As a result, they over-react to unwanted behaviors. People adopt a reactive approach when they should adopt a pro-active approach when dealing with pigs.

Pigs are unpredictable when it comes to behavior. They can easily get aggressive, depressed, bored, annoyed, irritated, and spoilt. That's why pig owners shouldn't keep their hopes up too high.

There will be times when their pig will charge at them, no matter how loving or loyal it is. When such situations occur, pig owners react in a bad way. They often scold or shout at their pig which doesn't help at all but makes the situation worst. Stay calm when dealing with pigs, even if it gets out of control. Adopt positive reinforcement strategies to handle your pig's attitude problems instead of snapping at it.

5) Caring for Aged Pigs

Caring for a piglet and an old pig is very tough. An aged pig is very sensitive, prone to illnesses, and needs extra attention from their owners. The older pigs need extensive care due to their age and health requirements. Taking care of an older pig will add some years to its life and help it fight different diseases.

Below is a list of considerations you will need to make if you have an aged pig at home.

Add more Proteins to Your Pig's Diet

Pigs are foodies but they will cut back on food when they are old. When older pigs eat less, they become thin and catch many illnesses. A pig's body needs pure strength to fight different illnesses and health conditions that may occur in old age. However, eating less food makes them sick and tired. Older pigs catch colds easily. They are more sensitive to weather changes. That's why they need a diet that is high in protein. Feed a greater quantity of protein rich diet to your pet. If it doesn't accept the food, do not force it to eat. You can consult a vet for your pig's eating problems.

A pig isn't supposed to be thin. When your old pig's appetite will drop, it will have a great effect on its health. If your old pig isn't doing too well on its recent feed, try changing it with a healthier feed. You may also need to consult with your vet before changing your pig's feed.

Pig Supplements

Older pigs get weaker and lack vital minerals and nutrients in their body. If your pig's health is dropping rapidly, see a vet and get your old fellow checked. Your vet will conduct a blood test on your pig which will show the deficiencies in your pig. If your pig is deficient in vitamins and minerals, your vet will prescribe certain supplements to make up for the deficiency. Some vets will suggest high-qualtiy pig feed rich in minerals and vitamins that will keep your old pig healthy. It is always best to go with a natural remedy like feeding green vegetables to your pig.

Feed Fresh Vegetables to your Old Pig

Pigs, no matter what age love to eat vegetables. An old pig needs more nutrition than a younger one. Older pigs tend to have digestive problems. They often get constipation which is not only painful but harmful for their health. With so many problems on hand, an older pig can take advantage from vegetables. Vegetables such as carrots, kale, red leaf lettuce, and spinach are packed with fibers. Fiber helps in solving digestive problems and keeps an older pig hydrated and active.

Smooth Surfaces

Older pigs have trouble walking on hard floors. Their bones and muscles weaken with time, resulting in poor control over their movements. Many older pigs tend to fall on floors easily. That's why it is important that the pigs be kept in places where the floor is soft like a carpet or a rug.

Older pigs also need more comforting beds and blankets. An old pig's care and a young pig's care is quite similar. You need to treat older pigs like babies because they are extremely sensitive.

Don't Leave them Unsupervised

Many old pig owners make a mistake of leaving their pigs alone. Old pigs are like children. They cannot take care of themselves and get hurt easily. Leaving an old pig home-alone is a huge mistake. They need constant attention and supervision to stay safe in their surroundings.

Weight

Pigs gain a lot of weight and fat on their bodies. Younger pigs do not have a problem carrying this weight because they are active and full of energy. However, an old pig fights with its weight problems as it interferes with its daily activities. An aged pig finds it hard to stand, walk, run, or do tricks. A lot of its health condition depends upon the way its owner handles it.

When you buy a pig, make sure you learn everything about the different stages of its life. The older pigs need a lot of care and attention from their owners. They will need to be fed the right amount of food so that they do not get sick. Some vets recommend different food for the older pigs as their body's requirements change.

Eyesight

A pig doesn't have good eyesight and it gets poorer with age. An old pig's eyesight is near blindness which means that it depends on its ears and nose. However, their almost blind sight will not cause major problems as their sense of hearing and smelling is excellent. If you change the place of your pig, it will take a little time to get used to the new place. Other than that, your old pig's eyesight is not going to be a big problem.

Exercise

Exercise is extremely essential for a pig's health; no matter how big or small. Older pigs also need exercise as it keeps their systems healthy. Aged pigs are not active and get irritable. They will usually lie around and not do anything at all. This is the most dangerous thing to your pig's health. It needs to get its daily dose of physical exercise.

Exercise keeps the heart healthy, body fit, blood running, lungs working, bones in good condition, and much more. That's why it is important that pig owners give time to their aged pet pigs. If they are being too lazy, involve them in some activity. Take them for a walk on a daily basis. Don't make your old pig run because it may fall and break its bones.

If you are having troubles taking your pig to a walk, make it chase you around the house with a treat in your hand. Think of new ways of making your old pig walk.

Overall Health

Older pigs incur many health problems which is natural given the age. However, these problems can be controlled by providing them with prudent care. Older pigs have digestive issues, urination problems, and irritable bowel movement. These pigs have troubles digesting and consuming food. That's why many older pigs stop eating.

Instead of feeding it forcefully, try adopting preventative measures that will root for the main problem. If your pig is having trouble eating and digesting food, contact your vet and get a medicine for it. There are many medicines available in the market that help in conditions like constipation, digestion, and urination for pigs.

An older pig will need to urinate and defecate several times a day. So, make sure that its litter box is within its reach.

Hydration

Water is extremely essential for older pigs because it keeps them hydrated and helps in improved food intake. Make sure your old buddy has clean water available at all times. If your pig likes apple or cranberry juice better, add it to water so that it consumes a greater amount.

Dental Care

The older the pig gets, the higher the chances of it losing its teeth. If you do not give proper attention to your pig's dental health from its earlier days, it is more likely to lose its teeth in the old age. Older pigs also get sores on the gum line.

Anesthetics

Older pigs do not require a great dose of anesthesia or fluorine gas. If your vet gives a higher dose to your aged pig, it will be life-threatening for it.

6) Caring for Baby Pigs

Taking care of piglets is very tough as they have special needs that need to be fulfilled. Baby pigs are very sensitive and need a lot of attention. It will need proper heating, feed, sleep, and much more. If you have bought a piglet, brace yourselves to face the toughest time of your life.

Lots of Love

A baby pig needs a lot of love and affection from the owner as it is separated from its mother. People that have bought baby pigs will need to keep an eye on them at all times. These sensitive pets are prone to catching different diseases your little pig friend will need a lot of cuddling and snuggling. If you can, keep your piglet in your room so that you can keep an eye at it.

Baby pigs that are separated from their mothers feel very uncomfortable and scared around others. Your piglet needs to feel relaxed and for that you will need to build a bond with it in its initial days. Once your piglet feels comfortable around you, you can start its training.

Bedding

Your new baby pet pig is sensitive to temperatures. It needs to stay in a warm place, that's why keep your little pig indoors. It is best to have a little bed for your pet pig inside your room. Get a soft bed for your baby pig that you can easily find in big stores and pet shops. You will also need to buy blankets for your piglet as pigs love to roll inside them. This will maintain their body temperature. If you turn-on the AC, make sure you have another place for your piglet. Keep heat-pads under your piglet's bed to keep it warm.

Food

If your piglet is younger than 3 weeks, you will need to bottle feed it. Piglets that young require a liquid based diet containing milk and formula. You can also add eggs in the milk to provide it with proper nutrition.

Baby pigs are prone to getting diarrhea. That's why it is extremely important that you feed the right quantity of feed which your vet will suggest. If your piglet gets diarrhea, you can give it a tablespoon of plain yoghurt mixed with milk.

It is not easy to bottle feed a piglet as it is not used to it. It will take time for the piglet to learn to drink through a feeder. To get in control of your pig, you will need to wrap it in a towel. Hold it under your arms and open its mouth using your finger.

Once the piglet opens its mouth, insert the teat inside it. Make sure you do not press the feeder and drop the milk in its airway. Drop a little milk in its mouth when it holds the teat properly. You will need to drop a few drops of milk in its mouth so that it knows its food. Try this for several times until your piglet learns to drink through a feeder.

Piglets need to be fed 5 times a day. You cannot leave the piglet with the feeder in its mouth, as it can be dangerous. Keep the piglet in your lap until it finishes drinking the milk.

At 5 weeks of age, your piglet will be all-set to eat dry kibbles and part solid food. You can now feed your piglet grains, bread, vegetables, and fruits.

Exercise

Exercise keeps a pig healthy. Younger pigs need to exercise to stay fit. When your piglet is comfortable around the house, take it outdoors for small intervals. Let it walk and run around the house and garden. Do not leave your baby pig alone because young pigs are extremely hyper. They love to chew on things that they find on the floor and try to get everything in their mouth, which can be really harmful for them.

If you cannot take them outdoors, make them chase you around the house. You can also hide toys in their bed and allow them to struggle to find it. Think of interesting and creative ways of giving your piglet its daily dose of physical exercise.

Rooting

Pigs need to root frequently and as piglets are really young, they are usually not left outdoors. To provide your piglet with its physical needs, buy an indoor rooting box for your piglet to dig into. Rooting will encourage a happy behavior in your piglet and will also help in its exercise.

Chapter 16: Use of Senses in Pigs

Pigs have been the most misunderstood animals. Since many people have started to show interest in them and choosing them as pets, their positive characteristics are coming to the fore-front. Pigs love mud baths and rooting, that doesn't mean they are dirty animals. They are one of the cleanest animals and love to stay neat. They take mud baths because they cannot sweat like humans and need to maintain their body temperature in warm seasons.

Pigs are intelligent and use their brain to a greater extent as compared to other house pets. They have strong senses that they take help from when moving around and finding food.

1) Sense of Smell

The strongest of all is the sense of smell in pigs. They move from one place to another with help of their extra-ordinary smelling power. Their snout is the most powerful when it comes to sense. Their sense of smell is so good that they sniff tidbits of food in garbage or under the blankets, etc. Their eye-sight might be very weak but their sense of smell makes up for it. That's why pig owners should not leave food items near the pig. They also use their snouts to smell underground truffles.

2) Sense of Hearing

Pigs have an extra-ordinary sense of hearing and use their ears to catch sounds and movements by predators. Mother Nature has classified pigs as a prey, that's why they need to be aware of the other animals that can harm them. A pig's sense of hearing also helps in its training process. When you ask your pet pig to do a trick using verbal actions, its excellent hearing senses will make things easier for you. In the wild, pigs rely on their sense of hearing and sense of smell to protect themselves from predators.

3) Sense of Sight

Pigs have poor sight and cannot see properly. They can only see things over a short distance. However, pigs have eyes on the sides of their nose that provide a panoramic view. Pigs use their sense of hearing and smelling to move and detect danger. Do not expect your pig to see hand actions from a far distance.

Pigs have dichromatic vision, which means that they can see two colors. Pigs can only slightly see red, blue, and green colors. They cannot see solid figures and lack the ability to focus on objects. This means that a pig has blurry vision. Pig owners should create such a living environment for them in which they feel comfortable to move from one place to another. The indoor are for a pig should not be chaotic, as the pig might have difficulty moving around.

4) Sense of Taste

Pigs have extra-ordinary eating habits as it can eat almost anything. If you drop tiny pieces of food on the floor, you will find your pig chewing on it. This is because pigs are omnivores and have 15,000 taste receptors on their tongue. They like to eat a combination of sweet and savory foods. That's why their sense of smell is extremely powerful. They detect harmful substances and food items with their sense of smell. Similarly, they also detect healthy food items for consumption.

5) Auditory Senses

A pig uses audio signals to communicate with other pigs and animals. They use auditory senses for various activities especially when communicating with other female pigs or attracting them. A pig makes different types of sounds based on their moods. For example; pigs growl when they are upset or angry, it makes a squealing sound when it is hungry or wants something, it oinks when it is in a good mood, etc.

Before buying a pig, one must conduct proper knowledge about the different sounds they make. This will help owners learn about their moods, feelings, and expressions. The sound that a pig makes is part of its language. They communicate with other pigs with help of these vocal expressions. Researchers have found that a pig makes 20 different types of sounds.

Young pigs make different sounds to communicate with their mothers. Male and female pigs also sing songs when they want to attract each other or send out a signal.

6) Sense of Touch

Pigs are social and affectionate, that's why they like being close to other pigs and humans. They make bodily contacts with humans and other animals to feel comfortable. Owning a pet pig means there will be a lot of snuggling, scratching, and physical contact. A pig loves to sleep in the bed, close to its owner. Their sense of touch is extremely alert.

Chapter 17: Pig Breeding

Home breeding pigs is better than any other breeding farm, etc. in a home environment; pigs feel more relaxed and comfortable. However, in a farm or enterprise, they feel stressed. Male and female pigs that are not neutered or spayed will feel the urge to mate. Female pigs go through a heat cycle every month and their first cycle starts when they are 170 - 220 days old. Females are mated with male pigs when they are cross their third heat cycle. Their vulva gets swollen and they pass mucus and blood from their vagina.

If you haven't already neutered or spayed your pig, you start to notice signs of excitement in your pig. This happens when the pig is on heat and needs to mate. Sexually active pigs are hard to handle, as they tend to become aggressive if not given an opportunity to mate.

1) Initial Exam

If you want more of those loving fellows roaming around the house, consider mating your pig. If you have a female pig, you will need to get a male pig and vice versa.

Before getting into a decision, you will need to take your pig to the vet. The vet will carefully examine the pig; check its medical records, and characteristics. This check-up will help you find out whether your pig is in a good condition to reproduce or not. If the vet tells you that the piglets born after mating will have some hereditary issues, it is better to weigh your options and then come to a decision.

2) Mating the Pig

When a pig reaches sexual maturity, it will think about two things; food and mating. If your pig is unneutered, you will face a lot of troubles as a pig gets very cranky and aggressive if its needs are not met. A pig on heat will mount almost anything including your leg. This can become extremely annoying and to avoid this behavior you can only choose the option of breeding.

If you have a male boar, you will need to get a healthy pig from the pet store. When on heat, a pig emits a very strong odor which is irritable to human nose. It will also be very protective and possessive about its lady. That's why owners that are trying to breed their pigs need to remain very careful and should stay away from female pigs when the male pig is around.

A female pig comes into heat every 21 days. During this period, the female pig will start to pee around the house in order to attract boars. Female pigs also get extremely cranky and moody during their heat cycle.

To impregnate a female pig, you'll need to be very careful of its heat cycle. Owners that want to mate their pigs are suggested to take note of their female pig's heat cycle.

3) Pregnancy – The Good News

Once you have mated your pigs, it is time to wait for the good news. A pig's pregnancy last up to 114 days. When a thin, yellow liquid starts to secrete from the mammary gland, you will know that it is about to give birth. When a pig reaches the end of its pregnancy, its teats get swollen and drag to the ground.

The female pig goes into nesting when the time is near. It will mostly feel uncomfortable and restless. Your pig will need a farrowing box in its personal pen to deliver its litter. The farrowing box is made to keep the little piglets inside and near their momma. Build a strong, narrow, and wide farrowing box so that both your pig and the piglets can accommodate in it. On average, the litter size remains 6-8; it can exceed to be 12-15 too.

If you are not an expert or lack experience, take your pregnant pig for a check-up to the vet. If you are having troubles travelling with it, call your vet home. It is always good to get professional advice in sensitive issue like these. You will need to ensure that you pregnant pig is in perfect shape to deliver. You might also want to know about the initial care of the piglets. The process of breeding is not that simple. It requires knowledge and expertise.

4) The Time is Here – Delivery Day

When the pregnant pig goes in its farrowing box, know that it is about to give birth any moment. When the pig is in labor, you will need to comfort her. Delivering 6-8 piglets is not easy. The pig will be feeling extremely uneasy. You can rub its belly gently to make it feel comfortable.

The things that you will need for the delivery of piglets include; scissors, clean towels, rubber gloves, and water. If you lack the experience and feel doubtful, make sure you get help from an expert breeder.

The first thing that comes out is the piglet's feet. Every piglet comes out in its sack that you will need to separate from it so that it could breathe. In most cases, the sack punctures on its own. You can make use of warm water to get the sack off of the piglets. If any piglet is having trouble breathing, use an aspirator.

Once the piglets are clean of mucus and the sack, tie its umbilical cord with a string and cut the rest of it. The piglets cannot be left alone with the sow during the birthing process. Gently pick the piglets after cleaning them and place them in a warm and dry box. When the birthing process is complete, you can leave the piglets with the mother.

5) What Happens in Complicated Deliveries?

Sometimes a sow will have complications while delivering the piglets. Firstly, make sure that you are present with your sow when it goes into labor. An uncomplicated delivery ends in approximately 2 hours. However, if a pregnant sow is 114 days into her pregnancy and still doesn't deliver on 115th day, it is time to contact a vet. When a sow refuses to deliver, complications arise. There is a high chance of the piglets suffocating inside. In such cases, certain conditions might indicate the pig needs medical assistance.

- You will need to contact a vet if your sow has crossed 115 pregnant days.
- You will need to contact the vet if your sow is discharging decayed placenta or discharge.
- You will need to contact your vet if your sow is straining and still not delivering the piglets.
- If there are prolonged intervals between the births of piglets, know that there is a problem.
- If your sow wasn't consuming enough food.
- If your sow is having trouble standing, moving, and breathing after the delivery.

Sows feel weak after delivering piglets. You can feed them a healthy stock to help them recover at a faster rate. Just like humans need strength from chicken stock when we are sick, pigs also need strength and energy from healthy foods.

6) Food for Pregnant Pigs

When your pig is pregnant, make sure you feed it high protein food so that it stays healthy and active. You will need to feed high quality food after the pregnancy as well. During the nursing period, the pig will spend most of their time inside the farrowing box, feeding its young piglets. Feeding the piglets its milk will take away a lot of energy from the pig's own body. She will need proper nutritious diet during her nursing period so that she can continue feeding her young ones.

7) Keep the Pen Warm

It is extremely important to maintain a warm temperature inside the pen. If the temperature of the surroundings is cold, install heat lamps and bulbs to make it warmer. Piglets require a temperature of 85 – 95 degrees. Make sure you are prepared with the heating systems before the piglets are birthed.

The temperature of the farrowing box should be warm because the piglets will be spending their initial days there. The warm temperature protects the piglets from catching different diseases and illnesses.

8) Bedding for Piglets

You will need to be extra careful with the bedding of the farrowing box. Sanitization is another thing that should be taken care of or else the piglets will fall ill. Clean the farrowing box every day and pick up the dirt. Make sure that the bedding remains dry and if you find that it is wet, change it immediately. Straw is the best bedding for baby pigs as it keeps them warm and dry.

9) Space is Crucial

When you are designing the farrowing box for the sow and the piglets, make sure you fulfill their requirements. Do not make the mistake of designing a small sized box, as it will put the piglets in danger. Piglets are tiny but the sows are huge and extremely heavy. A small farrowing box with less space will increase the chances of the piglets getting crushed under the mother.

Chapter 18: Interesting Facts about Pigs

Pigs are interesting animals. They love to play, run, cuddle, eat, and much more. These animals are extremely clever and use their brain to an extent that most animals can't. They are awesome companions and love to make friends.

Many people that know little about pigs would say bad things about them. This is because they are unaware of a pig's amazing qualities. Pigs make the best pets, as they are extremely loyal.

Let's read on to some interesting pig facts and get to know pig a little better.

- Pigs are intelligent animals and will start to recognize their name after 2 weeks of being born.
- Pigs have an extra-ordinary sense of smell and can smell things buried underground.
- When a pig curls its tail, it is happy.
- Pigs love water and are amazing swimmers.
- Pigs have been associated with gods in several cultures.
- Pigs are a sign of fertility in Chinese culture.
- Male pigs sing to attract female pigs.
- A mother pig's grunt tells the baby pigs that it is feeding time.
- Pigs are extremely intelligent and can learn complex tasks.
- Pigs are ranked at number fourth for being extremely intelligent.
- Pigs are loyal pets.
- Pigs love to socialize with other pigs.
- Pigs originated from Eurasian Wild boars.
- A pig can live up to 15 years.
- Pigs have been a part of art from 40, 000 years.

Chapter 19: The Little Friend

'Mini-Pig', 'Tea-Cup Pig', 'Micro Pig', etc, are all names given to a pig that is just about the size of a tea-cup. Some people might find it hard to believe but Tea-Cup Pigs do exist. However, the name given to them is just a marketing strategy.

If you are interested in buying a mini pig, make sure you know all about it.

1) Is Tea-Cup Pig for Real?

Many people have heard about mini pigs being the size of a tea-cup, but not everyone believes it. Tea-cup pigs are real and they surely exist. However, do not get fooled by the attractive names. Mini pigs are tiny pigs that are extremely adorable. These pigs are gaining popularity and many celebrities are buying them. Of course it is cute to see a pig fit in a tea-cup and that's what is driving people crazy.

The demand of a tea-cup pig is increasing day-by-day. These mini pigs are easy to play with and kids love to dress them up. Pigs have a number of qualities that make them desirable as pets. They are intelligent, social, loyal, clever, and what not. That's why many people now prefer pigs over other pets.

2) The Truth?

Tea-cup pigs exist but they do not stay micro sized forever. We all know how rapidly pigs grow and gain weight. The case with tea-cup pigs is that they are actually pot-bellied pigs that are underfed as piglets. These underfed pigs do not grow due to lack of nutrition and nourishment that they require. These pigs develop various health conditions and illnesses that can be a threat to their lives.

When the mini pig starts to grow and gain weight, it becomes huge. Tea-cup pigs can grow up to the size of normal pot bellied pigs that can no longer sleep with you in your bed. That's why it is extremely important for mini-pig owners to know that a mini-pig will not be the same size as they first bought it home. It is just a marketing gimmick to sell these little piglets.

3) Breeds & Sizes

There are several names for small sized pigs that float on the market. However, not every small pig belongs to the same breed. To get a better understanding of which mini pig to buy, read on to the sizes and breeds they are classified into.

Super Micro Pigs

These pigs are the tiniest and are less than 25lbs.

Micro Pigs

Micro pigs are the smallest sized pigs. Their weight ranges from 25-35lbs at the age of 18 months.

Tea-cup Pigs

Tea-cup pigs come after micro pigs. Their weight ranges from 35-55lbs at the age of 18 months.

Miniature Pigs

Miniature pigs are slightly bigger than the other pigs in this category. Their weight ranges from 65-85lbs as adults of 18 months.

A fully grown miniature pig will weigh approximately 40-60 pounds. To get a better idea of the growth of your mini pig, see its parents. Your mini pig will probably grow to the size of its parents. A full grown Vietnamese will weigh as much as 250 pounds which can be hard to manage if you were expecting your pig to stay mini forever. There are mainly two breeds of mini pigs; mini Vietnamese pot belly pigs and Juliana pigs.

4) Health

Your mini pig cannot be handled like a normal pig breed. This breed of pigs is very sensitive and need specialized care. When you buy a mini pig, make sure you get in touch with a vet that has experience with mini-pigs. At 4 weeks of age, your mini pig will need its first vaccination. When your mini pig turns 8 weeks old, it will need a booster vaccine. You will also need to de-worm your mini pig twice a year.

5) Skin

Mini pigs have sensitive skin just like other pig breeds. They cannot stay under the sun for long hours. Their skin can burn and dry off very easily. You will need to be extra careful with your mini pig's skin. Sunburn also causes irritation, redness, and skin infections in pigs. Provide your mini pig with adequate shade and shelter to protect them from the sun. Apply a sunscreen or skin lotion if your pig's skin becomes dry or burns from sunlight. You can also apply moisturizing creams after bathing your mini pig. This will protect its skin from skin infections and irritation.

6) Feeding Requirements

Mini pig feed is readily available on the market. Do not buy a normal pig feed for your mini pet, as it will not be suitable for its body type and weight. Feed your mini pig with youth food till the age of 1. Mini pigs love to eat vegetables and their diet contains a greater part of veggies. Fruits can also be added to their diet. However, fruits should be given in little quantity. Limit fruits to treats only.

Baby mini pigs will need 1/4th cup feed twice a day. When the mini pigs are 6-8 months old, they should be fed ½ cup, two times a day. A fully grown mini pig will need to be fed 1 cup twice a day. Mini pigs do not need to eat a lot of meat.

Don't feed cat or dog food to your mini pig as it contains high amounts of protein which will make your pig fat. Over-feeding a mini pig will make it grow faster. Weight also has negative effects on a mini pig's health.

7) Sufficient Water

Water is an essential part of a pig's life. Your pig will need to hydrate, so make sure you place a clean water bowl beside its food bowl. Pigs do not sweat, which means that they need to manage their body heat with help of water. Apart from drinking, your mini pig will need a water pool to soak itself in. Water will normalize its body temperature, helping it to stay cool in hot days of the summer.

8) Toilet Training

Pigs are clean animals that do not like to mess their homes, especially their sleeping area. Once you bring your mini pig home, you will need to potty-train it. You will need to buy a litter tray for your mini pig. Place this tray in a room and leave your pig in it after it has had its meal. Let the pig look for a place to poo in. Your mini pig is likely to poop in the tray. Repeat this process several times until your pig learns its toilet place. Choose a low-opening litter box for the little fellow or else it will have trouble getting in.

9) Housing

Pigs do not like change and after they have been separated from their mothers, they take time to adjust in a new environment. When you bring a mini pig home, make sure you give it plenty of time to make itself comfortable. Pig-proof your house before bringing it home. Clear off hazardous substances from your house, especially from the reach of your mini pig. Do not let your mini pig roam around the entire house. Keep them in a smaller area. Moreover, do not leave your mini pig unsupervised at any point in time. Mini pigs are so tiny that they can easily be lost in the house, under the bed, etc.

Flooring is another important thing to take care of before you get your mini pig home. A pig's hooves are hard and can easily slip on marble or tiled floors. That's why make sure that your mini pig doesn't walk on slippery surfaces or else it will fall and get badly injured. It is best to install carpets in the home to minimize the possibility of an accident or a fall.

A mini pig will love to sleep in a cozy bed. Use a basket or a tiny bed with blankets for your pig's bed. Make sure that the area you place its bed in is warm. Any damp surface will make your pig sick. You can also buy a dog kennel for your pig. Keep your mini pig's bed or crate in your room.

Clear off excess stuff and furniture from your home. Pigs love to explore and are curious by nature. They will try to touch everything in their surroundings. This is another way of getting to know the environment they live in. Remove any sharp or pointy things from the house.

10) Walking

Mini pigs love to walk. However, before you take them for a walk, make sure that you have trained them. Pigs are social animals but they can become aggressive if they see someone as a threat. Train your pig to walk on the leash. This will be rather easy due to the size and weight of the mini pig. Start leash and harness training when your mini pig is comfortable around you. Once it is trained to walk on the leash, you will be able to take it to the parks and streets.

There is another important thing to consider before taking your mini pig for a walk. Every state has different rules for a pet pig. Contact your area's council and get a registration license and permission. If you walk your pig in the parks without permission, you will need to pay a hefty amount of money as fine.

When walking your mini pig with a leash, be very careful. If your pig struggles or pulls on the leash, do not apply force or the leash will tighten. Mini pigs are tiny and can be easily hurt or injured. It is very important that mini pig owners first learn to walk their pets on a lead. Moreover, do not get angry at your pig if it doesn't learn the technique. Pigs do not take aggression too well. Train your mini pig with patience, tolerance, and consistency.

Always keep treats and toys with you while you are training your mini pig to walk. When you offer a treat to your pig when it follows your commands, it is motivated to listen to you every time. Moreover, make the use of verbal commands and hand signals to train your pig in a more effective way.

11) Neutering the Little One

It is better to buy neutered and spayed mini pigs from pet shops. Un-neutered male mini pigs develop a foul odor, get aggressive, and grow large tusks. Similarly, female mini pigs have abrupt mood swings, a monthly menstrual cycle, and peeing problems. You wouldn't want an un-neutered mini pig roaming around in your house. They can become very challenging and may hurt their owners or people around them. Spayed and neutered mini pigs do not get mammary cancers and other health problems.

12) Grooming the Mini Pig

Mini pigs are clean animals that don't like to get dirty. However, your mini pig will love to cover itself in mud. A mini pig's main grooming requirements are its ears, hooves, eyes, tusks, and skin. Mini pigs don't have a fur like other pet animals do. They have soft bristles that do not need extensive grooming or bathing. Maintaining a proper grooming schedule for your mini pig will make it look good and feel healthier.

Tools You will Require

There are certain tools that you will need to buy to meet your mini pig's grooming needs.

- Tweezers.
- Hoof trimmers.
- Soft hair brush.
- Moisturizing lotion.
- Mini pig gentle shampoo.
- Cleaning rag.
- Soft towel.
- Q-tips.
- Emery board.
- Tick powder.

Grooming Tips

- Brush your pig's skin to get rid of dirt and mud.
- Bathe your mini pig occasionally as its skin might get irritated due to excess bathing.
- Use normal temperature water to bathe your big.
- Use a garden hose to rinse it.
- Bathe your mini pigs in a small tub.
- Use a mild shampoo on your pig's skin.
- File or trim your mini pig's hooves.
- Use an emery board to trim the hooves.
- Groom your mini pig's eyes regularly as they develop a crud around their eyes which may look really messy.
- Use a soft damp cloth to wipe your mini pig's eyes.
- If you have an un-neutered mini pig, its tusks will grow rapidly. You will need to trim them once a year.
- It is best to visit a vet for tusk trimming.
- If your mini pig doesn't like the idea of a bath, keep it distracted with toys or treats.
- Use a non-slip bathing mat to avoid falls and accidents.
- Apply moisturizing lotion to your pig's skin after a bath.
- Dry your pig using a soft towel.
- Use a tick powder to get rid of fleas or lice on your mini pig.

13) Outdoor Spacing

Mini pigs will need outdoor spacing and yards to enjoy mud baths and rooting. Provide an outdoor space where your mini pig can dig and explore. Rooting will provide a good exercise to your mini pig. If you'll not provide an outdoor space for your mini pig, it will start to root inside the house and create a lot of mess. Provide a mud pool for your pig in the garden or the backyard. Your pig will love bathing in it. If a mini pig will not get to go outdoors, it will become destructive out of boredom. Outdoor space will also allow your mini pig to learn to defecate outside.

14) Exercise

Exercise is extremely essential for a mini pig. Adult mini pigs grow large and weigh quiet a lot. They will need regular walks in the outdoors. Exercise is not limited to walks. If you don't have time, you can play with your mini pig inside the home as well. Hide treats and toys in your pig's blankets. This will give your pig good exercise. Moreover, regular physical activities will keep your pig healthy. Mini pigs are extremely smart and clever. They are quick learners and will learn tricks and techniques very quickly. Train your mini pig to walk on the leash, so that it is easier for you to control them.

15) Socializing Your Mini Pig

Mini pigs love to socialize and make new friends. When you bring a mini pig home, you will soon learn that they will crave for your attention. They will spend most of their time with their owners or around people. However, if you have other pets or children in your home, train your mini pig to behave with them.

Pigs are unpredictable and can get aggressive if they feel threatened. Mini pigs go well with cats but dogs can be a problem. Do not leave your mini pig unsupervised with kids or other pets. Pigs get depressed and aggressive if left alone. Give proper time to your pig or else it will become destructive.

Chapter 20: Pet Pig's Attitude Defined!

A pig's personality varies in different situations. However, pigs are usually affectionate and social animals that crave their owner's attention. Let's find out the common behavioral traits of a pig that will help you bond with your pig in a better way.

1) Know when to stop

Pigs are social and will like to play and cuddle. However, a pig owner must be aware that sometimes a pig has mood swings. When a pig is upset or feels threatened, it reacts badly. These mood swings are absolutely normal and just like humans, pigs need their space. If you force a playing routine on your pig, it will give you warning signs. Your pig might get uneasy during a play or a social meeting with friends and family. You should notice your pig's body language and learn what they mean so that you don't get attacked by your own pet. When you pig isn't comfortable in playing or meeting people, do not force it. When pigs are forced onto something, they snap and become aggressive.

2) Do not Mess with its Sleeping Area

Just like humans hate giving their bed to someone else, pig do too. The behavioral traits of a pig are very similar to that of humans and that's why they are perfect pets for humans.

Pigs are extremely territorial and don't like anyone coming in their sleeping area. If you let strangers touch your pig's sleeping area or bed, it will become furious. Why so? Pigs are prey animals, that's why they hide in safe spots in the wild and it is their natural instinct. So, when someone touches their bed, their smelling sense catches it. They become extremely aggressive and start to growl. They feel that their hiding spot is no more a hiding place. A pig might charge or bite at people in aggression.

This reaction of your pig isn't abnormal. It is just a self-defense tactic to keep itself safe from invaders and enemies. That's why it is extremely important for pig owners to know that your pig's bedding area is not be messed with.

3) Strengthen Your Bond with Your Pet Pig

Pigs are very likeable animals when kept as pets. These social animals will become loyal to their owners and protect them at any cost. Many people love to keep dogs as pets because they are loyal, loving, and extremely intelligent. However, pigs have better loyalty and intelligence rankings than a dog.

If treated and trained well, pigs become the best pets. Bonding with your pet pig should start at an early age, so that your pig becomes your best friend. It is extremely important to know that if you let your pig become possessive about you, it will cause troubles for you. Over-protective pigs are the ones that have never been away from their owners. This can be a huge problem when you leave your pig alone in the home. Your pig will not only become aggressive, but it might never act the same way. Again, this is not your pig's fault.

Pig owners should know that a pig needs to be kept in a limit. Do not stay with your pig for the entire day, if it gets used to being around you all the time, it will not like when you leave for a little while. If you have other family members at home, divide time so that your pig gets used to different people and not just you.

Your pig will bond with you in a better way if you train it well when it is just a piglet. Piglets will adapt to your rules easily. The way you treat your pig will reflect on its behavior and the relationship it has with you.

4) Your Pig Needs a Friend of its Own Kind

If you think your pig is happy having you, you are wrong. A pig is a living being and like humans, these animals need a friend of their kind to stay happy. If you are planning on buying a pig a pet, make it two. A pig will share a deeper bond with a fellow pig than a human. Getting two pigs is wiser than getting one. If you are buying a male and a female pig, make sure they are neutered or spayed. Un-spayed or un-neutered pigs can become a problem for you as they will mate and rapidly multiply in number. They also have aggression problems, so it is better to get a neutered pair.

Living with a fellow pig will make your pig learn social skills that will be helpful in bonding them with other pets and people.

5) *Do not get Scared with all that Snapping*

Pigs tend to get moody and aggressive due to their instinctive nature. They are territorial, dominant, and will snap at anyone they find a threat. Many pig owners complain that their pet pigs are snapping and charging at strangers. The only reason your pig may get snappy is because it is not happy with its surroundings. This usually happens when a pig is bored, socialized with strangers, and left alone.

To make the snapping attitude go away, you will need to tell the pig that you are the boss of the house. This behavior can be controlled with the help of behavioral training exercises. When your pig snaps unexpectedly, use verbal commands to get its behavior under control. However, do not yell at your pig in aggression as the situation might head in some other direction. A pig is trained with consistency, patience, and repetition. Other than that, you cannot force your pig to listen to you.

Chapter 21: Taking Care of an Over-Weight Pig

A huge problem that many pet pig owners face is their pig getting obese or over-weight. Being over-weight is a sign of poor health. A pig gets obese due to its lifestyle and eating habits. Pigs are animals and on top of it; omnivores. They will eat anything that they find and still feel the need to graze.

The responsibility of a pig's health falls entirely on its owner or caretaker. Pigs have a tendency to put on fat and that's why most of the pigs are prone to catching many diseases. So, how do you keep a check on your pig's lifestyle? How do you make your pig lose those extra pounds? Below are some guidelines and tips to take care of your over-weight pig.

1) Healthy Diet

The thing that most affects a pig's health is eating fatty food, especially a commercial pig feed. Commercial pig food consists of a lot of fat and carbohydrates that are harmful for a pig's health. However, feeding a limited quantity of commercial food to your pig will not create health problems.

It is important that you keep a track of your pig's eating habits. Pigs love to eat and nothing can stop them from chewing onto food items in the bin. As an owner, you are responsible to keep food items and bins away from your pet pig.

If you are noticing that your pig is gaining a lot of fat and is getting lazy, reduce the amount of food and increase the frequency of servings. If you feed two bowls of commercial pig feed to your pig, replace commercial food with fresh vegetables. Serve little commercial feed once a day.

Do not cut back on your pig's food. It is not healthy to let your pig starve. It is going to lose weight in an unhealthy way. You can allow your pig to graze in your lawn all day and not feed it as much food. This is another healthy way to maintain your pig's health. If your pig is gaining lots of weight by eating commercial pig feed, replace the feed with a healthier pig food or home-cooked meals.

2) Exercise is a Must

Many pigs that get over-weight have trouble walking and moving. These obese pigs will lie down in one place all day long, which will make their health worse. Exercise plays a vital role in a pig's life. A pig's physique is naturally fat and a pig stays healthy that way. However, gaining extra pounds creates a variety of health risks for a pig.

If you take your over-weight pig for frequent walks and engage it in physical activities, it is less likely to gain that much weight. Losing weight is not a magical process. It takes time for a pig to get back in shape. Be patient, take your pig for walks, play with your pig, let it swim and dig in the mud, and your pig will be fit.

3) Treat or No Treat?

Many owners feed their pig excessive treats which makes them gain a lot of weight. Treats should be kept healthy and should only be offered in a limited quantity. Offer treats only during the training process of your pig. It is important for the owners to know that treats are not a replacement for food. Do not feed treats to your pig all the time, as it will make it fat. If you are feeding a lot of treats, make sure you reduce the amount of food for the day.

The best treats are in the form of vegetables and fruits; only limited veggies and fruits that are harmless for a pig. You can replace treats with another form of reward during your pig's training session. For example; instead of offering treats, give a pat on your pig's back, offer a play-toy, or simply snuggle with it to show your appreciation.

4) Health Concerns for Over-Weight Pigs

It is easy to over-feed your pig because it is fond of food. Your pig will not know when to stop eating. To keep your pig healthy, you will need to fix its diet and routine. A pig can gain an extra 100 pounds if fed fatty foods.

Being over-weight is not only unappealing to look at but it is also very hazardous for a pig's health. Over-weight pigs feel pain in their body and are prone to falling and slipping. The different health concerns in an over-weight pig are:

Deafness

When a pig is obese, the fat accumulates around the air canal which makes it hard for it to hear sounds and it becomes deaf.

Blindness

Fat also accumulates under a pig's eyes and makes it go blind. A pig's vision is already very poor but fat can make the situation worse.

Bad Behavior

When a pig gets over-weight, its body starts to ache. It feels pain in its mass and bones. Due to the intense pain in its entire body, a pig often becomes aggressive and moody. A pig is not a dull and lazy animal. It is extremely active and curious. It loves to explore and run around the house. When a pig gains a lot of weight, it becomes harder for it to stand or even walk. When a pig is bound to stay at one place due to its weight condition, it becomes frustrated.

Pigs are easily bored as well. That's another reason for them to become snappy and aggressive. Lying in one spot, deprived of physical activity is a torture for a pig. That's why it reacts by exhibiting bad behavior. Another way a pig expresses its anger is by chewing on the carpet or anything that is kept near it. The pig needs to engage itself in activities to keep itself from getting bored. The chewing habit is a bad one, as it will ruin your furniture and other stuff in the house. You can give chew toys to your over-weight pig so that it doesn't ruin your house.

Fractures and Joint Diseases

Arthritis, fractures, hip dysplasia, and joint diseases are all the problems that an over-weight pig is exposed to. Fractures are very common in over-weight pigs as their bones are not capable to handle that amount of weight. When an over-weight pig tries to walk or stand, it often slips. This happens because an obese pig will not be able to balance its weight on its legs. The bones of the legs are pressed with hundreds of pounds, as a result they break.

Hip dysplasia in pigs often occurs due to weight problems. A pig that is extremely fat will be prone to bone, tissue, and muscle damage. To keep your pig healthy and safe from fractures, you will need to take them for regular physical exercise. If you can't take your pig outdoors, engage in a playing activity inside the home.

Heart Conditions

The way a human heart gets affected to the fat accumulation inside the arteries, similarly a pig's arteries also get blocked due to fat. Heart diseases are common amongst pigs with weight problems. Coronary heart disease majorly affects a pig's health and in worst cases, the pig dies.

5) *Talk to a Vet*

If your pig is gaining a lot of weight and is falling under the symptoms of depression and anxiety, visit a vet. A vet will monitor your pig, its weight and size to give you suggestions on weight control. Moreover, do not change your pig's feed on your own. First, consult with a vet that will give you a better idea of the type of food your pig needs. A vet will also help you develop a plan for your pig. This weight-loss plan will allow you to control your pig's weight by adopting healthy and effective methods.

6) Old Pigs Die Early

A preventative approach towards your pig's diet and lifestyle will help you keep it healthy. A pig that becomes over-weight does not live a long life. There are numerous health problems that occur in an over-weight pig. These pigs also go under severe depression due to lack of activity that they require.

If you want your pig to live a long life, choose a high-quality pig feed that doesn't have a lot of fat. Moreover, feed your pet two times a day. Add a lot of veggies to your pig's diet and try to feed it home-cooked meals. The benefit of a home-cooked meal is that the owner knows what's going in it.

The commercial hog feed available in the market is full of fat and harmful substances that could be a threat to your pig's life. Commercial feed contains high amounts of corn syrup and preservatives that creates health problems in pigs.

Some pig feed available on the market also contains plants, seed, and feeds that are dangerous for pigs. You can consult with your vet or a pig nutritionist to get suggestions on pig feed. A commercial pig feed is usually packed with lots of ingredients that you cannot keep a track of. It is strongly suggested that pig owners look into the ingredients in the pig feed they buy.

Pigs will eat almost anything but that doesn't mean you can offer them whatever there is. When you feed commercial food to your pig, it will eat it fondly. It is the responsibility of the owner to check the ingredients and avoid feeding anything that is harmful or toxic.

The life of your pigs is in your hands. This means that you will need to be very careful of the way you grow your pigs. Your pig needs an active lifestyle to stay fit and healthy.

7) Do not keep Your Pig on Grazing Alone

Pigs are active eaters and will chew on the grass all day long. However, do not confuse your pig's grazing habit with food. Grass alone will not be enough for your pig as it is an omnivore. It needs both protein and herbs to survive and stay healthy. Many pig owners let their pigs graze in the backyard all day long and cut back on their meals.

Feed proper meals to your pig because grazing will not provide it with sufficient energy, vitamins, minerals, and essential nutrients that its body requires.

Chapter 22: Confined Spaces & Pigs

It is extremely important for pig owners to understand a pig's behavior when it is kept in confined spaces. In the wild, pigs like to roam in open spaces, which provide them with sufficient exercise. When pigs are kept in apartment rooms or pens, they become destructive and often go under stress. They switch-on their defensive mode which is not quite attractive.

1) Behavioral Issues

The biggest problem with pigs in confined spaces is that they become very aggressive and exhibit bad behavior. It is not fair to blame it on the pig as it is not designed to live in small spaces. A pig is an active animal that loves to play and run. A pig that is forced to live in a confined room doesn't get its daily dose of exercise. This exercise deprived pig gets upset and starts to act up.

It is extremely normal for a pig to get aggressive if it is left to suffer in a small area. When you let such a pig out, it will snap at you or in worst cases become violent. Pigs have the tendency to become violent. Before you keep your pig in a confined space, remember that it will bring out its negative side.

2) Stress, Anxiety, and Depression

Pigs are social animals and they crave attention from their owners. That's why they don't like the idea of being left alone. Pigs that are forced to live in a room, deprived of their basic needs will get depressed. Pigs that live in a dull and boring enclosure get depressed easily. This is a common problem with pigs in captivity.

Before you get a pig and leave it to suffer in a small room, learn about its psychology. Pigs are outdoor animals and don't respond well to small areas or homes. A pig will need grazing area and the backyard to dig in the mud. When a pig doesn't get enough human attention, it is highly stressed out.

3) Boredom

Bored pigs are the most destructive ones. If you leave your pig in a small area, it will not get enough exercise or playtime. This will give you pig nothing to get engaged in. the pigs in confined areas do not get to have fun. A pig that is given proper outdoors area will be happier and healthier. Provide your pig with a normal lifestyle; let it engage in physical activities, playtime, swimming, mud baths, and much more.

4) Health Problems

Many health problems in pigs occur because they are forced to settle in a poor environment. The pigs in confined rooms or apartments will develop bone diseases, heart diseases, skin infections, and much more. A healthy pig is the one that is exposed to the outdoors and given ample opportunities to exercise. Household pigs have a shorter lifespan as compared to the outdoor pigs. Pigs in the wild live in open lands and forests. It is their natural instinct to play, walk, and exercise. Moreover, the food of a confined pig doesn't get digested, causing several illnesses, constipation, and much more.

5) Let them out!

If you have a small apartment and you have bought a pig as pet, make sure you let it out every day. Little outdoors exercise is essential for a pig to stay healthy. You can also engage in play with your pig and dedicate a few hours of your day to interact with your pig. You can also give toys to your pig so that it can stay engaged without getting bored.

6) A Sweet Escape

Pigs in confinement are more likely to escape. A pig will not miss any chance to run free out of a place that is depriving it of everything that it needs. If you don't have enough time or you stay out of home for long hours, do not choose to buy a pig.

7) Aggression

When you will leave your pig in a small area where it cannot run freely, it will become aggressive. Pigs have a loving nature and they love to socialize and make friends. However, they become extremely aggressive and angry when they are left alone. Aggression in pigs is something you wouldn't want to see. Angry pigs grunt, bite, and may potentially harm their owners or anyone that comes near them.

8) Fixing the Environment for the Pig

If your pig is showing signs of depression, aggression, and bad behavior, look around and find the solution. Pigs usually stay in a good mood. However, there are certain things and situations that make them behave badly. A pig is majorly affected by its environment. It is genetically engineered to live in open spaces with mud and water. It loves to run around and when confined to a small room, a pig can become the opposite of what it is.

If your room is too little for the pig, take it for a little walk in the park or your neighborhood. If your state rules don't allow a pig to be outdoors, walk it in a bigger room or your own backyard. You can also provide it with some activity or exercise. Keep your pig engaged in physical activities that boosts up its mind and health.

Provide your pig with a social environment that satisfies its natural instincts. That's the only way you can have a well-mannered pig. Owners and guardians of pigs need to be sensible and provide their pigs with the space they require. It is not a behavioral issue of pigs but an issue from the owner's side. Resolving such issues requires knowledge about the animal that every owner should know prior to the purchase.

Conclusion

Pigs are harmless animals that are extremely conscious of their hygiene. There is a great misconception amongst people about pigs and that's the reason no one ever considered them as household pets. However, the people that have owned pigs have cleared this misbelieve and this book is also a contribution to it.

Pigs have numerous qualities that over-shadow some of their odd behavioral traits. They are extremely intelligent, smart, clean, clever, curious, loyal, friendly, protective, affectionate, playful, and so on. There are several great things that come along with this pet.

It is extremely important to buy a pig from a reputable breeder. A pig that is bred in a poor environment will develop several diseases and behavioral issues. After making the decision of buying a pig, you will need to prepare your home to become a perfect home for a fat friend.

A pig has several desirable qualities that make them better pets than any other animal. These highly intelligent animals learn tricks and commands quickly. Pigs are trainable and will obey their guardian's orders. Pigs also follow voice and hand signals, which are an important part of their training process. A pig's intelligence is rated as higher than a dog's, which means that with help of training, pigs will learn almost anything.

A very likeable quality of a pig is that it is extremely loyal to its owners and guardians. It protects its territory and its owners from threats and can be harsh to strangers breaking in the house without permission. A pig is very similar to dog and if dogs can be kept as pets, then why not pigs?

Pigs do not like to be left alone. They crave attention, love, and affection from their owners and when left alone, they tend to get aggressive. Aggressive pigs are dangerous as they can hurt others. Again, there is nothing unusual about a pig getting aggressive.

There is a way of reacting to your pig's anger tantrum. Never in a million years try to force your pig or yell at it. Pigs don't react well to aggressive behavior. You can control your pig's aggression problems with the help of different training techniques. Positive reinforcement is the only way your pet pig is going to calm down and behave.

A pig is a long-term friend that will live up to 12-15 years. This pet can become challenging at times but for the most part, pigs are affectionate animals that need love and some snuggles. To turn your pig into a respectful and obedient pet, you will need to invest time in training it from a small age. Keep the training sessions short; be repetitive, consistent, and patient during the entire process.

A pig is a perfect pet if you have time to give it the love it needs. It will not only be your best friend, but will also protect you in times of need. There are many pros to petting a pig than cons. That's what makes pigs admirable and appealing as pets.

Published by IMB Publishing 2015

25631589R00103

Printed in Great Britain
by Amazon